FROM CONFUSION TO CLARITY:

THE COMPLETE CAREER COUNSELING HANDBOOK FOR PARENTS AND STUDENTS (9TH TO 12TH GRADE)

Divya Majhi

MBA, Green Belt Certified Global Career Counsellor from Univariety, UCLA

BlueRose ONE.com
Stories Matter
NewDelhi • London

BLUEROSE PUBLISHERS
India | U.K.

For permissions requests or inquiries regarding this publication, please contact:

BLUEROSE PUBLISHERS
www.BlueRoseONE.com
info@bluerosepublishers.com
+91 8882 898 898
+4407342408967

ISBN: 978-93-6783-388-9

Cover Design: Aman Sharma
Typesetting: Pooja Sharma

First Edition: February 2025

About the author

Divya Majhi, a renowned Global Career Counselor, holds an MBA from Universal Business School and a Green Belt certification from GCC University, UCLA Extension. She brings extensive expertise in content writing, data analysis, and sales and marketing, having worked with international businesses across diverse sectors.

As the founder of Destiny Craafters (www.destinycraafters.com), Divya empowers parents and students to make well-informed career decisions. Her experience as a school counselor for grades 10 to 12 provides her with a deep understanding of students' needs, enabling personalized and impactful guidance.

Through a comprehensive and results-oriented approach, Divya ensures individuals confidently navigate their academic and career paths. Share your feedback and connect at divyammajhi@gmail.com.

Acknowledgment

I would like to Show my heartfelt Gratitude to Appreciate to everyone who has been Very Important and a Big Support in this journey of making **From Confusion to Clarity: The Complete Career Counseling Handbook for Parents and Students (9th to 12th Grade)** with Me.

First and foremost, I want to express my gratitude to my spiritual guru, who has taught us and shown a direction to spread love and affection towards others and also to help other human beings. This is a lifelong lesson I will never forget. Those are the values she has always taught to me . It is this specific teaching that motivated me to write this book—to offer knowledge that I have and help students and parents who are on the wrong track or are stuck in the career decision making process.

A heartfelt thank you to my husband, Madhav Majhi, who has consistently provided me with inspiration and motivation and Support in Every Way. I have been Pregnant Through My Journey of this Book writing and He is the one who was always beside me to help me in my needs. His support and faith in me have been crucial at every stage of the journey.

Many many Thanks To my mom and dad, your love and sacrifices have molded me into the person I am now. Your support during every stage of my life from childhood to this stage that I am in, has consistently been my source of strength, and for that, I am eternally grateful to my Beloved Parents.

I am extremely thankful to my friend Shruti, who consistently had faith in me and inspired me to pursue my dreams and kept sharing insightful ideas she had from her experience . Your encouragement has been a beacon of hope, and I value your unwavering belief in my efforts.

Next Of Course are the parents and Students i have come across and interacted with I would also like to express my gratitude towards them. It's them that with so many queries and the challenges they faced they inspired me to write this book for Self You are the reason I selected this route to address the inquiries that numerous individuals encounter in their quest for career clarity.

I also want to show my gratitude towards my beloved Cats, my Kids, Ruby and Prince & Also My baby Who has been supporting me even though he/she has still not entered this world. Their unwavering presence of all my kids has provided me with lots of energy and boosted my happiness, and I feel that connection with me has strengthened me and throughout the most challenging moments of this journey.

With sincere gratitude,

Divya Majhi

Preface

Today, students and parents face many choices and uncertainties about education and careers. **From Confusion to Clarity: The Complete Career Counseling Handbook for Parents and Students (9th to 12th Grade) will help** students & parents discover their strengths, explore career best possible options, and guide parents to support their children with confidence during this critical phase.

This book is inspired by the stories and questions of students and parents, reflecting my passion for accessible career counseling. I am deeply thankful to my spiritual guru, my husband Madhav Majhi, my friend Shruti, my parents, and my pets Ruby and Prince for their unwavering support and encouragement.

With gratitude,

Divya Majhi

Contents

Who can use this book and how?
Very important

This book is designed to be a comprehensive guide for students, parents, and educators, helping them navigate the complexities of career selection, academic decisions, and personal development. Here's how each group can benefit:

1. Parents

- **How to Use**: Parents can refer to this book to gain insights into how they can support their children's career journey. The sections on *streams, subject selection, preschool curriculum*, and *career maps* help parents understand the various academic and career paths their children might take. The guidance on choosing the right curriculum, dealing with confusion around dropping subjects (like math), and understanding the role of career counseling will empower parents to make informed decisions for their children's future. The *psychometric assessments* and *profile building* tips also help parents recognize the importance of understanding their child's strengths and interests.

- **Key Sections for Parents**:
    - Choosing the right curriculum for preschool kids
    - Understanding career maps
    - The importance of career counselors
    - Psychometric assessments
    - Supporting students' subject choices and career decisions

2. Students

- **How to Use**: Students can use this book to gain clarity on how to plan their academic and career paths. Sections like *career maps, subject selection,* and *entrance exams* provide clear, step-by-step guides to help students make well-informed decisions. The *SOP (Statement of Purpose)* and *resume building* templates will help students prepare for college applications and future job opportunities. The inclusion of *new age careers, study abroad guides,* and *career options in various fields* ensures that students have access to the latest trends and opportunities available to them.
- **Key Sections for Students**:
    - Subject selection under different streams
    - Entrance exams

- Career maps and degree/diploma options
- Writing an SOP and personal story
- Study abroad guidance
- Career options in science, commerce, humanities, and defense

3. Educators and School Counselors

- **How to Use**: Educators and school counselors can use this book as a valuable resource to guide students in selecting the right subjects, making informed career choices, and preparing for future academic opportunities. The book provides templates like *SWOT analysis* and *performance trackers* to help monitor student progress. It also offers strategies for effectively communicating the role of a career counselor and supporting students' personal and academic growth.
- **Key Sections for Educators**:
  - Supporting students' needs and guiding decision-making
  - Career counseling tips
  - Templates for tracking student progress
  - Building a student's profile for future success

Key Features of the Book:

- **Career Mapping**: Helps students and parents visualize a path to success, including new-age careers and traditional options.
- **Psychometric Assessments**: Clarifies how these tests can help in understanding interests, strengths, and personality.
- **Ready-Made Templates**: Provides practical tools like goal-setting and SWOT analysis for students to create personalized career plans.
- **Study Abroad & Entrance Exam Guides**: Offers essential information on applying abroad, writing SOPs, and preparing for entrance exams.

This book is a valuable resource for anyone looking to make informed decisions about education and career paths, whether you're a student planning your future, a parent guiding your child, or an educator supporting students through their academic journey.

Steps to finalise career

Choosing a career is one of the most important decisions that can shape a student's future. It requires a clear understanding of their Strength, Weakness, Opportunity and Interest . This simple guide will help students explore and select the right career options.

1. SWOT Analysis of the Student

The first step in career planning is conducting a **SWOT (Strengths, Weaknesses, Opportunities, and Threats) analysis**. This helps in identifying the student's internal and external factors that may influence their career decision.

- **Strengths**: What are the student's key skills and strengths (e.g., analytical abilities, creativity, leadership)?
- **Weaknesses**: Areas where the student might need improvement (e.g., time management, communication skills).
- **Opportunities**: External factors that can be leveraged (e.g., industry trends, available educational opportunities).
- **Threats**: Potential challenges or barriers (e.g., market saturation in certain fields, lack of resources).

This self-assessment helps create a foundation for career decision-making.

2. Psychometric Test

After conducting a SWOT analysis, the Second step is to take a psychometric assessment test. These tests evaluate a student's personality, cognitive abilities, interests, and preferences. They are a powerful tool to understand a student's natural inclinations, abilities, and behavior patterns, which are important to identify suitable career options.

Psychometric tests can assess a persons :

- **Kinesthetic Intelligence**, it tells how strong is the person's mind and body coordination. Few people with good Kinesthetics intelligence are Musicians, carpenters, grinding machine operators, crane operators, dancers, etc
- **Linguistic Intelligence,** it tells about hold on the language like how good are you at reading, writing, speaking even the sign language is a part of this intelligence like technical writer, translators, foreign language speakers / teacher, editors etc.
- **Spatial Intelligence,** it tells about the ability to identify objects accurately, change and recreate images, and recognize how shapes and objects relate to each other, for example people like Pilot, Architects, Mechanical Drafters, computer engineers etc.

3. Analyze the Test Results and Correlate with SWOT Findings

After completing the psychometric assessment test, the results should be carefully analyzed and matched with the findings from the SWOT analysis. This step helps in matching the student's personal traits and strengths with the career options that are most suited to them. And further by just comparing the insights from both the SWOT analysis and psychometric test, you can identify patterns and validate potential career pathways.

For example:

- If a student's SWOT analysis highlights strong leadership skills and the psychometric test indicates a high level of extraversion, careers in management or public relations could be a good fit.
- If a student's strengths lie in creative problem-solving and their test results show a preference for artistic endeavors, careers in design, advertising, or media might be ideal.

4. Finalize Chosen Career Options

Once the analysis is complete, the next step is to narrow down the career options based on the combined insights from the SWOT and psychometric test. It's important to focus on careers that align with both the student's personal strengths and long-term interests.

Key considerations include:

- **Skills alignment**: Does the student have the necessary skills or is there a need for development?
- **Interest alignment**: Does the student genuinely enjoy the work involved in the chosen field?
- **Values alignment**: Does the career path align with the student's personal values (e.g., work-life balance, job security)?

5. Research the Finalized Career Options

Once the career options are narrowed down, it is essential to conduct thorough **research** on the final choices. This includes understanding the career's pros and cons, job prospects, required qualifications, and future trends.

Things to research:

- **Pros and cons of the career**: What are the advantages and challenges in this career?
- **Job market and growth potential**: Is there a demand for this career, and what are the growth opportunities?
- **Qualifications and skills required**: What degrees, diplomas, or certifications are necessary?
- **Entrance exams and application procedures**: What exams need to be cleared to pursue this

career (e.g., IIT-JEE for engineering, CLAT for law)?

- **Feasibility**: Is the career realistic based on personal circumstances, available resources, and the current job market?

6. Choose a Career Wisely and Prepare a Career Map

The Last step is to choose the **career path wisely based on the research**, SWOT analysis, and personal preferences. Once the career is finalized, it's time to work on a **Career Map** that outlines the journey from education to employment.

Career Map includes:

- A Short-term goal: A short term goal could be immediate like subject selection or which entrance exams to prepare for.
- A Long-term goal: A Long term goal could be the ultimate objectives for example completing a degree, securing a job in a specific company, or what will i do after my graduations? etc.
- Action plan: To prepare for a step-by-step guide on how to achieve these goals for example studying for exams, internships, skill development or participating in any summer camp, internship program etc.

Additionally, students should create a **yearly plan** that includes important milestones such as:

- Preparing for entrance exams (timelines and study schedules)
- Researching colleges or training institutions
- Pursuing internships or practical experiences to enhance skills
- Building a professional network and resume

So why is this topic so important?

Choosing a career without doing a psychometric test can lead to poor decisions. However, a decision based on scientific findings allows for a clearer evaluation & vision of all possible and suitable career options.

What is profile building for K-12 students?

What is Profile Building?

Profile building refers to the process of creating and enhancing a student's personal and academic profile, focusing on showcasing their strengths, skills, achievements, and interests in a way that aligns with their future academic and career goals. This process helps students stand out in college applications, job searches, or scholarship programs by highlighting their unique qualities and accomplishments.

For **K-12 students**, profile building is a continuous process that involves the development of various aspects of the student's life, including their academic performance, extracurricular activities, volunteer work, skills, and personal qualities. A well-rounded profile demonstrates not only academic excellence but also leadership, initiative, and personal growth, which can be particularly important for admissions to universities or scholarships.

Profile Building for K-12 Students

For K-12 students, profile building starts early and evolves over time as students gain more experiences and mature. The goal is to help students present themselves in the best possible light when the time comes for them to apply to colleges, universities, or enter the job market. A profile of a student is good when it is started at a very early stage of life right from Grade 5th or 6th.

Here are key components of **profile building for K-12 students**:

1. Academic Performance

- **Grades & Coursework:** A student's profile is largely based on their consistently high academic performance. This entails achieving academic success, subject mastery, and a high GPA for K–12 students.
- **Test Results:** Results on school and high school standardized tests, including entrance exams

2. Extracurricular Activities

- **Sports & Clubs:** A well-rounded student is demonstrated by their active involvement in extracurricular activities like clubs, sports, theater, music, and debating.
- **Positions of Leadership**: Having leadership roles in extracurricular activities at school and high school, such as club president, team captain, or class president, adds a lot of value to the profile and demonstrates traits like initiative, accountability, and the capacity to lead and manage others.

3. Volunteer Work & Community Service

- **Volunteering and social impact initiatives** are powerful ways for students to showcase their character and values. Active participation in community service highlights a sense of responsibility, empathy, and a commitment to making a difference in the lives of others. Whether through local projects like teaching underprivileged children, organizing cleanliness drives, tree plantation drives or global initiatives addressing climate change, these efforts reflect a student's dedication to societal betterment. Such experiences not only enrich personal growth but are also highly valued by colleges, universities, and employers, as they demonstrate leadership, compassion, and the ability to contribute meaningfully to a larger cause.

4. Skills Development

- **Soft Skills**: In addition to academic skills, students should also focus on developing soft skills like communication, time management, problem-solving, critical thinking, and collaboration. These skills are essential for success in higher education and in every position in future including when a student is applying for university applications.
- **Technical Skills**: Depending on their interests, students can also develop technical skills, such as coding, graphic design, public speaking, or digital marketing. These skills enhance the profile and make students more competitive right from University application to finding a good job.

5. **Personal Achievements & Recognition**

- **Awards & Honors**: A student profile should show Recognition for academic or extracurricular achievements, if they have won a competition, or received an academic award, or being selected as a leader in any program, should be highlighted as part of a student's profile while applying to universities.
- **Special Projects**: Any independent projects or research that a student undertakes, such as science fairs, art exhibitions, or entrepreneurial ventures etc should be documented.

6. **Building a Strong Online Presence**

- **Social Media and Portfolios**: For High School and Graduates a well-curated online presence is essential for example having a LinkedIn profile is a must, a personal website if required or an online portfolio that showcases their work for those into artwork, writing, coding projects) can be a powerful way to highlight achievements.
- **Online Courses or Certifications**: Taking online courses or earning certifications in subjects of interest for self improvement and enhancing skills.

7. **Professional Networks & Mentorship**

- **Building Relationships**: Encouraging students to network with teachers, mentors, and professionals in fields of interest can lead to valuable guidance, internship opportunities, and recommendations in the future.

- **Mentorship**: Establishing relationships with mentors who can guide students on their academic and career journeys also strengthens their profile, as it indicates a proactive approach to personal growth. For example if you like photography, or any skill based careers. Coding, or Marketing, video editing etc.

8. Career Exploration & Internships (For Older Students)

- **Internships**: For high school students (especially in grades 11-12), internships or work experiences in fields of interest are excellent ways to build a profile.
- **Career Shadowing**: For students who are not yet ready for internships, career shadowing programs or online career exploration opportunities can be beneficial for gaining insight into different fields, Or even Summer Camp can be very helpful.

Profile-building opportunities available for students in India across various categories:

Academic Competitions and Olympiads

1. SOF Olympiads: Science, Mathematics, English, Cyber, and General Knowledge Olympiads. https://sofworld.org/
2. National Talent Search Examination (NTSE): Scholarship program for academically gifted students. https://ncert.nic.in/national-talent-examination.php
3. Indian National Olympiads: Organized by HBCSE in subjects like Mathematics, Physics, Chemistry, Biology, and Astronomy. https://iapt.org.in/
4. Spell Bee India: English language and vocabulary competition. https://indiaspellingbee.com/competition.php

Coding and STEM Competition

1. **TCS iON IntelliGem:** Challenges students in areas like digital awareness, creativity, and global citizenship.
2. **WhiteHat Jr Hackathon:** Coding and app development competition for school students.

3. **RoboCup Junior India:** Robotics competition focusing on coding and AI. https://www.rcjindia.com/competition

Public Speaking and Debate Forums

1. **Model United Nations (MUN):** Platforms like Indian International MUN for honing debate and diplomacy skills.
2. **World Individual Debating & Public Speaking Championships:** An international competition that includes debate, persuasive speaking, and other formats
3. **National Speech and Debate Association:** In Public Forum Debate, students work in pairs of two to debate both sides of a topic. Public Forum is one of the most popular events and is a great entry point for new students and judges.

Science (ISRO) YUVIKA - YUva VIgyani KAryakram (Young Scientist Programme) only for 9th grade students

How Profile Building Helps K-12 Students:

- **University Applications**: A strong, well-rounded profile helps K-12 students stand out in college or university applications. Admissions committees often look for students who not only excel academically but also demonstrate leadership, creativity, and a commitment to their community.

- **Scholarships & Awards**: A solid profile is key to winning scholarships, awards, and recognition in academic and extracurricular areas.
- **Career Preparation**: Building a profile early prepares students for success in their careers by helping them develop skills, experience, and interests that align with their future goals.

In conclusion, **profile building for K-12 students** is an ongoing process that involves developing academic, personal, and extracurricular aspects of a student's life. By focusing on strengths, achievements, and growth areas, students can build a profile that not only prepares them for college applications but also sets them up for long-term success in their careers.

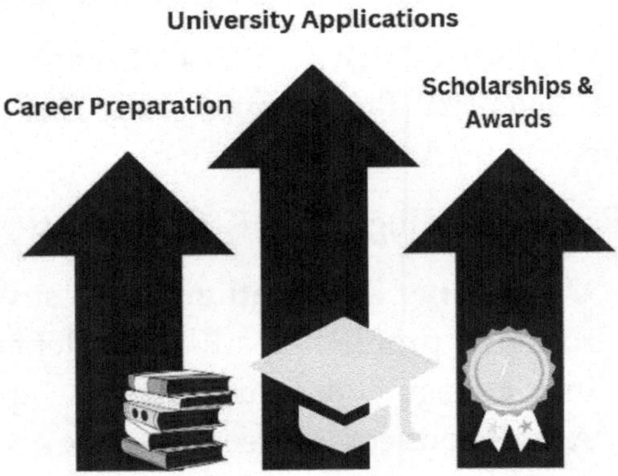

Why is a career counselor important & their role in decision-making?

A **career counselor** plays a critical role in guiding students and individuals through the often overwhelming and complex process of career decision-making. Their importance cannot be overstated, as they provide valuable support, resources, and guidance to help individuals make informed decisions about their education, career paths, and future goals.

Here's why a career counselor is essential, and how they contribute to the decision-making process:

1. Expert Guidance and Knowledge

The expertise that career counselors bring to the table is detailed. They are well-versed in a wide range of career options, market trends, educational prerequisites, and the abilities required for success in various domains. This aids students in navigating the wide range of options at their disposal.

- **Role in Decision making :** By providing information on job prospects, educational opportunities, and career trends, career counselors assist students in making well-informed decisions. They guarantee that decisions are founded on accurate, current information by offering clarity on possible career paths based on the student's strengths, interests, and long-term objectives.

2. Objective and Unbiased Perspective

Parents, teachers, friends, and even students themselves may have differing views when it comes to choosing a career. Without any outside influences, a career counselor provides an unbiased, objective viewpoint, concentrating only on what is best for the student.

- **Role in Decision making :** Career counselors can assist students in evaluating their options objectively and reducing their susceptibility to the opinions of others by offering an independent point of view. This gives the student the ability to make choices that fit their objectives, values, and interests.

3. Personalized Career Assessment

Every student is Different, with different strengths, weaknesses, and aspirations. A career counselor uses various tools, such as **psychometric tests, career assessments, and one-on-one counseling sessions**, to understand the individual's personality, skills, and preferences.

- **Role in Decision-Making**: By analyzing the results of these assessments, counselors help students gain a deeper knowledge of their aptitudes and interests, which in turn assists in selecting the right career options. This personalized approach ensures that career choices are tailored to the individual's strengths and long-term success.

4. Clarifying Career Options and Pathways

The wide range of career options available today can be overwhelming. Career counselors help students explore and understand different career fields, industries, and educational pathways. They provide detailed information about the scope of various careers, required qualifications, potential job growth, and salary expectations.

- **Role in Decision-Making**: Counselors help students narrow down their options by evaluating the pros and cons of each career path. They highlight factors like job stability, future growth opportunities, and personal satisfaction, enabling students to make well-informed choices.

5. Helping with Goal Setting and Planning

In addition to helping students choose a career, a career counselor helps them set both short- and long-term goals to help them reach their career goals. In order to help students lay a solid foundation for their chosen career, this involves offering advice on course selection, skill development, internships, and extracurricular activities.

- **Role in Decision-Making**: By helping students develop clear, actionable plans, career counselors ensure that the decisions made today align with future ambitions. This creates a roadmap for success, guiding students toward their goals step by step.

6. Emotional Support and Motivation

The process of choosing a career can be stressful, especially when students feel uncertain about their future. Career counselors provide emotional support and encouragement throughout the decision-making process, helping students overcome doubts and build confidence in their choices.

- **Role in Decision-Making**: A counselor's reassurance and motivational guidance are key to reducing anxiety and indecision. With a career counselor's help, students can feel more confident in their decisions, which ultimately leads to better outcomes in their educational and career journeys.

7. Addressing Parental Concerns and Expectations

Parents have a big influence on career choices in many cultures. However, students may become confused due to parental pressure or conflicting viewpoints. By assisting parents in understanding their child's interests and strengths and offering advice on how to support their goals, a career counselor can mediate these conflicts.

- **Role in Decision-Making**: Career counselors work with both students and parents to ensure alignment between the child's goals and family expectations. This ensures that students feel supported and understood, which can lead to a more harmonious decision-making process.

8. Providing Resources and Networking Opportunities

Numerous resources are available to career counselors, such as networking platforms, internships, scholarships, and employment opportunities. They give information about pertinent events, career fairs, and educational institutions and assist students in making connections with professionals in their chosen fields.

- **Role in Decision-Making**: These resources allow students to make more informed career choices by providing real-world insights into the job market. Networking opportunities with professionals and mentors can also help students understand the practical realities of their chosen career.

9. Continuous Support and Guidance

Choosing a major and applying for jobs are only two aspects of choosing a career. A career counselor offers students ongoing assistance and direction as they advance in their academic or professional endeavors. This entails creating resumes, honing interview techniques, and making plans for career advancement.

- **Role in Decision-Making**: Career counselors act as mentors throughout a student's academic life, ensuring that they stay on track, remain motivated, and adapt their career plans as new opportunities and challenges arise.

Ultimately, a career counselor helps students build a clear vision for their future, empowering them to make confident, well-researched decisions that will set them on the path to success.

To Book an Appointment with me for career counseling : Write to me on divyammajhi@gmail.com

What is a career map and its importance?

It's always good to have known our path. The path to knowing how to reach goals. Hence, Career Maps play a very vital role in every one's career. But for now we are talking about the aspiring students. Career Maps are pathways that help students to decide and evaluate an accurate roadmap for reaching their goals. . It outlines their aspirations, potential education and training pathways, skill development needs, and long-term career options.

A typical Career Map Includes::

- **Career goals**: Short-term (1-3 years) and long-term (5-10 years).
- **Educational pathways**: Courses, programs, or degrees needed.
- **Skill requirements**: Skills they need to develop (e.g., technical, soft skills).
- **Action steps**: Key milestones and timelines (e.g., exams, internships, certifications).

Importance of Career Map is:

- **Clarity of Goals**:
    - Helps students understand their interests and align their academic choices with long-term career aspirations.

    - Avoids confusion about which field to pursue.

- **Guided Decision-Making**:
    - Provides a roadmap for selecting the right subjects, courses, and colleges/universities.
    - Reduces the risk of choosing irrelevant or mismatched career paths.
- **Focus and Motivation**:
    - Gives students a sense of purpose and motivation to work towards their goals.
    - Encourages them to remain proactive and goal-oriented.
- **Skill Development**:
    - Identifies areas where students need to build their competencies, whether technical skills, communication skills, or leadership qualities.
- **Preparation for Future Challenges**:
    - Helps students anticipate challenges and prepare strategies to overcome them, such as entrance exams, competitive markets, or financial constraints.

Template Of Career Map Below :

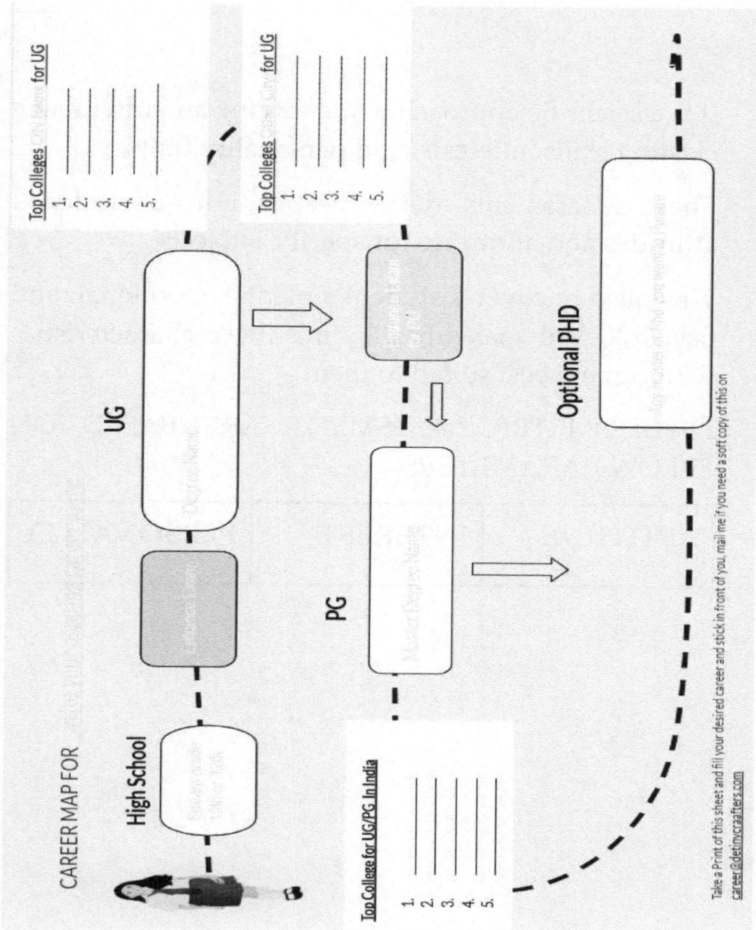

What is a psychometric assessment?

It is a scientific approach to identifying an individual's existing skills, interests, and personality traits.

These assessments delve deeper into a student's attitudes and aptitudes for specific subjects.

They also uncover a student's mental, emotional, and psychological makeup, aligning these characteristics with careers best suited to them.

PSYCHOMETRIC aSSESMENT ARE BASED ON BELOW PARAMETERS

APTITUDE	INTEREST	PERSONALITY

What is the importance and types of psychometric assessment?

Psychometric assessments play a crucial role in career guidance and personal development by providing an objective and scientific understanding of an individual's abilities, interests, and personality traits. Here's why they are important:

1. **Highlights Strengths and Weaknesses**: Identifies a student's key abilities, areas for improvement, and hidden talents.
2. **Aligns Career Choices**: Matches a student's aptitude, interests, and personality to suitable career options.
3. **Provides Objectivity**: Offers unbiased insights, free from societal or parental pressures.
4. **Identifies Aptitudes**: Assesses skills like problem-solving, reasoning, and communication to suggest areas of excellence.
5. **Explores Personality**: Reveals traits like leadership potential, introversion, or extroversion, aligning careers with natural tendencies.
6. **Guides Skill Development**: Pinpoints skill gaps to focus on for career readiness.

7. **Clarifies Academic Pathways**: Helps students choose appropriate subjects, streams, and courses.
8. **Boosts Confidence**: Validates career decisions with scientific data, enhancing self-assurance.
9. **Supports Emotional Well-Being**: Reduces stress by fostering self-awareness and understanding psychological makeup.
10. **Provides Backup Options**: Suggests alternative career paths, ensuring flexibility and preparedness.

Types of Psychometric assessment ?

1. **Stream Selector Test**:
2. Assesses a student's interests, strengths, and aptitudes to recommend the most suitable academic stream (e.g., Science, Commerce, Arts).
3. It ensures alignment between the student's capabilities and their chosen field of study.
4. **Learning Styles Test**:
5. Identifies the preferred way a student absorbs and retains information, such as visual, auditory, or kinesthetic learning.
6. Helps tailor study methods for more effective learning and academic success.
7. **Personality Type Test**:

8. Examines traits like introversion, extroversion, decision-making style, and work preferences.
9. Guides students toward career choices that resonate with their personality.
10. **Ideal Career Test**:
11. Matches a student's interests, skills, and values with potential career paths.
12. Offers personalized recommendations for professions that align with their unique profile.
13. **Multiple Intelligences Test**:
14. Explores different types of intelligence, such as logical, linguistic, musical, or interpersonal.
15. Encourages students to focus on their strongest intelligences to identify suitable career options.

To Book an Appointment with me for career counseling : Write to me on divyammajhi@gmail.com

Or Scan my website : www.destinycraafters.com

SCAN ME !

Choose a right curriculum for parents who are confused for there preschool kids :

Types of Curriculum currently in India :

India Schools offer both Indian and International Syllabus

- CBSE: Central Board of Secondary Education
- ICSE: The Indian Certificate of Secondary Education
- IB: International Baccalaureate
- IGCSE: International General Certificate of Secondary Education (IGCSE) Cambridge University
- State Board: State Government Recognized Board.

CBSE (Central Board of Secondary Education):

The CBSE is a national education board in India, known for its centralized and structured syllabus. It places a strong emphasis on science, mathematics, and technology, offering a comprehensive curriculum for students. Schools following the CBSE system prepare students for key national exams like the All India Secondary School Examination (AISSE) for class 10 and the All India Senior School Certificate Examination (AISSCE) for class 12. This board is widely recognized across India and forms the foundation for many competitive exams.

Pros:

- National recognition and widely accepted across India and by universities.
- Well-structured syllabus focusing on science, mathematics, and technology.
- Application-based learning in subjects like science.
- Aligned with national competitive exams (JEE, NEET, etc.).
- Centralized and uniform education system across India.

Cons:

Limited emphasis on arts and humanities.

- High pressure due to exam-oriented approach.
- Rigid structure with less flexibility for non-traditional subjects.

ICSE (Indian Certificate of Secondary Education):

The Council for the Indian School Certificate Examinations (CISCE) oversees the ICSE board, which provides a thorough and well-rounded education with a particular emphasis on literature and English. It offers a thorough curriculum covering topics like the humanities, arts, and sciences. Students are prepared for both domestic and foreign higher education through ICSE's comprehensive approach. The board promotes all-around growth with an emphasis on research and critical thinking.

Pros:

- In-depth, comprehensive curriculum with a strong focus on English, science, and humanities.
- Holistic development emphasizing critical thinking, research, and analysis.
- International recognition, beneficial for students planning to study abroad.
- Strong emphasis on English language proficiency.

Cons:

- Higher difficulty level and extensive coursework may be challenging for some students.
- Less focus on technical subjects compared to CBSE.
- Generally more expensive due to better resources and materials.

IB (International Baccalaureate):

The IB is an international educational foundation offering three programs: PYP, MYP, and DP, designed to foster a global perspective and interdisciplinary learning. It emphasizes critical thinking, student development, and inquiry-based learning. The IB curriculum is recognized by universities worldwide for its rigor and holistic approach. It prepares students for higher education with a focus on global challenges and ethical responsibility.

Pros:

- Promotes global perspective and international-mindedness, ideal for students aiming for higher education abroad.
- Encourages inquiry-based learning, critical thinking, and independent research.
- Emphasizes well-rounded development in intellectual, emotional, and ethical areas.
- Diverse assessment methods (projects, presentations, exams) making learning more interactive.

Cons:

- High cost of the program and additional activities.
- Intense workload, especially in the Diploma Programme (DP).
- Limited availability of IB schools in some regions.
- Less focus on regional educational needs and local context.

IGCSE (International General Certificate of Secondary Education):

The IGCSE, offered by Cambridge Assessment International Education (CAIE), is an international curriculum popular among students planning to study abroad. It covers a wide range of subjects, with a focus on practical learning, global perspectives, and critical thinking. The IGCSE curriculum is comparable to CBSE/ICSE in terms of subjects and grading, but it emphasizes a more flexible and interdisciplinary approach.

Pros:

- International recognition, widely accepted by global universities.
- Offers flexibility with a wide range of subjects, allowing students to tailor their learning.
- Focus on practical learning and real-life applications.
- Balanced curriculum with both academic and creative subjects.

Cons:

- Expensive tuition fees.
- Stressful due to heavy emphasis on internal assessments and projects.
- Limited availability of IGCSE schools in smaller towns.

- Transition issues for students switching from Indian boards to IGCSE.

State Board:

State Boards are education boards recognized by state governments, each with its own syllabus and exams. The curriculum emphasizes regional languages, state history, and culture, tailored to local needs. It follows traditional learning methods and often prioritizes regional subjects, offering a more localized educational experience.

Pros:

- Regionally relevant syllabus, including local languages, history, and culture.
- More affordable, making it accessible to a wider range of students.
- Familiarity with the system, as students are used to state-specific exams.

Cons:

- Limited scope with a greater focus on rote learning.
- Variation in quality due to lack of uniformity in syllabus across states.
- Less global recognition compared to CBSE, ICSE, or IGCSE.
- Less emphasis on developing critical thinking and problem-solving skills.

Every curriculum has unique benefits and difficulties, and a student's best option will rely on their learning preferences, goals, and the resources at their disposal. The curriculum must be chosen with the goals and academic requirements of the student in mind.

The following template will assist you in selecting the right school or high school. Please refer to the example column for better understanding. Note that the school names provided are fictional and not associated with any real institutions.Choose the template wisely.

How to Choose Right High School or School	**Explanation**	**Parent Comment**	**School 1**	**School 2**	**Example (Springfield High School) This is just example**
If its closer to home (Rating) 1 to 10	if closure choose 10, 9 etc				8/10 (Parent Comments: Springfield High is just a 10-minute drive from home, making it convenient for daily commutes.)
FEES / Flexibility (Rating) 1 to 10	high fees to low				Rating: 6/10 (Comment : The tuition is moderately priced

					compared to nearby schools, but there are limited scholarship options available.)
Academics (Rating) 1 to 10	The school's academic program and flexibility				Rating 7/10 Comment : The school has a strong academic reputation, with a high percentage of students going to college and several Advanced Placement (AP) courses offered.
Extracurricular activities (Rating) 1 to 10	The range of clubs, sports teams, and artistic pursuits offered				Rating: 7/10 Comments : Offers a variety of clubs and sports, though some programs are underfunded and have

					fewer participants.
Safety measures (Rating) 1 to 10	The safety measures in place at the school				Rating: 9/10 The school has a robust safety plan, including security personnel and regular drills.
Word of mouth / Google Review (Rating) 1 to 10	Feedback from other people about the school				Rating: 7/10 Generally positive reviews from parents and students, but some concerns about administration responsiveness.
Total of Rating	**Total the rating whichever is higher can help you decide**				**44**

Visit and observe schools	Your Comments				Visited during a school day; classes appeared engaged, and students seemed happy and involved.
Students Observation	Students Comments				Students were friendly and willing to discuss their experiences. Many spoke highly of the teachers and support staff.
School History					Established over 50 years ago, Springfield High has a long tradition of academic excellence and community involvement.

Any Negative News					Recently, there were reports of a bullying incident that raised concerns among parents. However, the school has taken steps to address this issue with new initiatives and support systems.

Subject streams available in India:

Currently in India If we see the distributions and students are choosing more Science and Arts stream according to the latest study by the Education Ministry. Below is one of the article printed in The Print where we see "Science and arts are consistently the most popular streams in the last 10 years. Students who opted for science and arts streams have increased from 31 per cent (for both science and arts) in 2012 to 42 per cent and 40 per cent respectively in 2022," the study said.

More students have also been opting for vocational courses,In terms of absolute numbers, 30.9 lakh students took the arts stream in 2012, which went up to 40 lakh in 2022. The science stream had 30.7 lakh students in 2012, which increased to 42 lakh in 2022. As many as 13.7 lakh students had taken the commerce stream in 2012 and 14.4 lakh pupils in 2022.

"The data shows that students' choices in the last decade have been based on job availability and the market outlook. Science and technology being the biggest job generator has attracted most students. Numbers not growing in commerce is a surprise for us as well because given the job opportunities in the finance sector and number of students opting for management studies, the numbers should have increased," said an education ministry official, who was a part of the study.

(Source: https://theprint.in/india/education/only-14-students-took-commerce-in-last-10-years-more-arts-science-takers-says-govt-study/1604442/)

Streams most students opt every year is as below :

SCIENCE	ARTS / HUMANITIES	COMMERCE

A snap from the news below:

ThePrint
Empower the news you trust and depend on
ThePrint SUBSCRIBE
POLITICS GOVERNANCE ECONOMY DEFENCE INDIA GROUND REPORTS OPINION EVENTS VIDEO MORE LOGIN
Education

Only 14% students took commerce in last 10 years, more arts & science takers, says govt study

The education ministry study also said that more students opted for science in Andhra Pradesh, Telangana & Tamil Nadu, while takers for arts were more in Gujarat, Punjab & Rajasthan.

KRITIKA SHARMA 31 May, 2023 06:52 pm IST

Commerce:

As the foundation of any economy, commerce is a dynamic field that centers on trade, business, finance, and economics. It develops students' analytical and decision-making abilities while supplying them with information about market dynamics, business operations, and financial systems. A solid basis for comprehending the intricacies of both domestic and international markets is provided by courses like accounting, economics, and business studies. From established professions like banking and chartered accounting to cutting-edge industries like digital marketing, e-commerce, and fintech, a degree in commerce opens doors to a wide range of career options. For students who want to influence the business world, commerce is a great option because it combines theoretical understanding with real-world application.

Below are some careers from Commerce, Also a brief of How AI can Impact this Stream.

- ❖ Accountancy:

Career Pathway :

- ➢ **Class 12th**: Commerce with Accountancy.
- ➢ **UG**: Bachelor of Commerce (B.Com) with specialization in Accountancy.
- ➢ **PG**: Master of Commerce (M.Com) in Financial Accounting or Chartered Accountancy (CA).
- ➢ **Professional Certifications**: Certified Management Accountant (CMA), Certified Public Accountant (CPA), Financial Data Analyst certifications.

Career Options & Role you enter after Commerce with Accountancy :

- Accountant
- Auditor

- Tax Consultant
- Financial Controller
- Cost Accountant
- Chief Financial Officer (CFO)
- Finance Manager
- Treasury Manager
- Management Accountant
- Financial Data Analyst
- Blockchain Accountant
- Accounting Automation Specialist
- Forensic Accountant
- Tax Technology Specialist
- Predictive Analytics Specialist
- Corporate Advisor
- Risk Analyst
- Mergers & Acquisitions Specialist
- Business Valuation Expert
- Financial Consultant
- Accounting Educator/Professor
- Research Analyst in Finance
- Chartered Accountant (CA)
- Certified Management Accountant (CMA)

- Certified Public Accountant (CPA)
- Certified Internal Auditor (CIA)
- Financial Planning Specialist (CFP)

New-Age Careers in Accountancy with AI Integration

The role of AI is rapidly transforming accountancy, leading to new-age career opportunities that blend traditional accounting expertise with advanced technology skills.

- ❖ **Financial Data Analyst**
  - ➢ Role: Analyze and interpret large datasets using AI tools to provide actionable insights into financial performance and market trends.
  - ➢ AI Impact: Tools like Tableau, Power BI, and machine learning algorithms are used to predict financial outcomes and automate report generation.
- ❖ **AI-Powered Forensic Accountant**
  - ➢ Role: Use AI algorithms to detect fraudulent transactions and ensure compliance with financial regulations.
  - ➢ AI Impact: AI can analyze vast volumes of transactions in real time, identify anomalies, and flag suspicious activities for investigation.

- **Tax Technology Specialist**
  - Role: Develop and manage AI-driven tax software for accurate tax compliance and reporting.
  - AI Impact: AI-powered tax platforms like Avalara and TurboTax automate tax calculations, compliance checks, and filing.
- **Accounting Automation Specialist**
  - Role: Implement and manage AI-driven accounting software like QuickBooks, Xero, or SAP to automate bookkeeping and financial reporting.
  - AI Impact: AI eliminates repetitive tasks such as data entry, enabling accountants to focus on strategic decision-making.
- **Blockchain Accountant**
  - Role: Leverage blockchain technology to ensure transparent and tamper-proof financial records.
  - AI Impact: Blockchain, combined with AI, enhances security, streamlines audits, and ensures the integrity of financial data.

- **Predictive Analytics Specialist**
    - Role: Use AI tools to forecast financial trends, budget requirements, and market opportunities.
    - AI Impact: Machine learning algorithms enable precise financial predictions and scenario planning.
- **AI-Driven Financial Controller**
    - Role: Oversee financial operations using AI for budgeting, forecasting, and compliance monitoring.
    - AI Impact: AI can optimize cash flow management, reduce errors in financial statements, and ensure regulatory adherence.
- Business Studies Or Management Studies

Career Pathway:

1. **Class 12th**: Commerce with Business Studies.
2. **UG**: Bachelor of Business Administration (BBA) or B.Com in Business Studies.
3. **PG**: Master of Business Administration (MBA) in General Management, Marketing, or Operations
4. **Professional Certifications**: Project Management Professional (PMP), Six Sigma Certification.

Career Options & Role you enter after Commerce with Business Management :

- Business Analyst
- Operations Manager
- Entrepreneur
- Business Development Manager
- Project Manager
- Marketing Manager
- Sales Manager
- Product Manager
- Supply Chain Manager
- Human Resource Manager
- Financial Analyst
- Management Consultant
- Brand Manager
- Retail Manager
- Customer Relationship Manager
- Risk Manager
- Corporate Trainer
- E-commerce Manager
- International Business Manager
- Public Relations Manager
- Strategy Consultant

- Event Manager
- Data Analyst
- Business Operations Consultant
- Investment Banker

New-Age Careers in Business and Management with AI Integration

AI integration in the following business roles leads to enhanced efficiency, data-driven insights, automation, and better decision-making. Here's how AI impacts each of these roles:

1. **Business Analyst**
    - AI-driven data analysis tools provide real-time insights, automate reporting, and identify trends and patterns for faster decision-making.
2. **Operations Manager**
    - AI optimizes workflows, predictive maintenance, and resource allocation, improving operational efficiency and reducing costs.
3. **Entrepreneur**
    - AI helps in market research, business model innovation, customer insights, and automating business processes to scale operations efficiently.

4. **Business Development Manager**
    - AI tools assist in lead generation, customer segmentation, predictive analytics, and personalized sales strategies, enhancing business growth.
5. **Project Manager**
    - AI aids in project planning, resource allocation, risk management, and timeline optimization using predictive analytics and project management tools.
6. **Marketing Manager**
    - AI helps with customer behavior analysis, personalized marketing, automation of ad campaigns, and improving customer targeting through predictive modeling.
7. **Sales Manager**
    - AI tools support lead scoring, customer behavior prediction, sales forecasting, and performance analytics, improving sales efficiency.
8. **Product Manager**
    - AI assists in analyzing user feedback, product performance data, market trends, and automating product development workflows.

9. **Supply Chain Manager**
    - AI enhances demand forecasting, inventory optimization, route planning, and logistics through predictive analytics and automation.
10. **Human Resource Manager**
    - AI streamlines recruitment, talent management, employee engagement, and performance monitoring through automation and data analysis.
11. **Financial Analyst**
    - AI tools provide real-time financial analysis, automate data collection, and use predictive modeling for investment decisions and risk assessments.
12. **Management Consultant**
    - AI enhances decision-making, market research, and strategy formulation by analyzing large datasets and identifying emerging trends.
13. **Brand Manager**
    - AI aids in monitoring brand sentiment, customer feedback analysis, and market trends to refine branding strategies and campaign performance.

14. **Retail Manager**
    - AI optimizes inventory management, customer behavior analysis, sales forecasting, and personalized shopping experiences in retail.
15. **Customer Relationship Manager**
    - AI enhances customer service by automating responses, providing personalized recommendations, and predicting customer needs for better engagement.
16. **Risk Manager**
    - AI helps in identifying, assessing, and mitigating risks using predictive analytics, real-time data analysis, and automating compliance checks.
17. **Corporate Trainer**
    - AI enabled personalized learning experiences, adaptive training programs, and performance tracking through learning management systems (LMS).
18. **E-commerce Manager**
    - AI drives personalized customer experiences, predictive inventory management, automated customer support, and dynamic pricing strategies.

19. **International Business Manager**
    - AI helps in market entry analysis, risk management, cross-cultural customer insights, and forecasting trends in global markets.
20. **Public Relations Manager**
    - AI assists in sentiment analysis, crisis management, content generation, and predicting media trends for better PR strategies.
21. **Strategy Consultant**
    - AI supports data-driven strategy formulation, market analysis, competitive intelligence, and scenario planning through advanced analytics.
22. **Event Manager**
    - AI helps with event personalization, guest engagement, predictive analytics for event planning, and post-event analysis.
23. **Data Analyst**
    - AI enhances data collection, cleaning, and analysis, while offering predictive insights, trend identification, and automation of reports.

24. **Business Operations Consultant**
    - AI supports operations optimization, process automation, cost reduction strategies, and real-time analytics for business improvements.
25. **Investment Banker**
    - AI helps with market trend analysis, risk assessment, fraud detection, and automating routine financial tasks for faster deal-making.

❖ Economics

Career Pathway:

1. **Class 12th**: Commerce with Economics.
2. **UG**: Bachelor of Arts (B.A.) in Economics or Bachelor of Science (B.Sc.) in Economics.
3. **PG**: Master of Arts (M.A.) in Economics or Master of Science (M.Sc.) in Economics.
4. **Advanced Studies**: M.Phil. or Ph.D. in Economics.

Career Options & Role you enter after Commerce with Economics:

- Economist
- Financial Analyst
- Policy Analyst
- Market Research Analyst

- Economic Consultant
- Investment Analyst
- Data Analyst
- Risk Analyst
- Public Policy Advisor
- Government Economic Advisor
- Business Analyst
- International Trade Specialist
- Labor Economist
- Environmental Economist
- Development Economist
- Actuary
- Agricultural Economist
- Health Economist
- Education Economist
- Quantitative Analyst
- Corporate Strategy Analyst
- Urban and Regional Planner
- Corporate Finance Manager
- Monetary Policy Advisor
- Financial Planner

❖ **Finance**

Career Pathway:

1. **Class 12th**: Commerce with Finance or Mathematics.
2. **UG**: B.Com or BBA with Finance specialization.
3. **PG**: MBA in Finance, M.Com in Finance, or Master of Finance (MFin).
4. **Professional Certifications**: Chartered Financial Analyst (CFA), Financial Risk Manager (FRM).

Here are some career options and roles you can enter after studying **Commerce with Finance**:

1. **Chartered Accountant (CA)**
    - **Role:** Financial Auditor, Tax Consultant, Accounting Manager
    - Specialize in auditing, tax planning, and financial reporting.
2. **Financial Analyst**
    - **Role:** Investment Analyst, Portfolio Manager, Equity Research Analyst
    - Analyze financial data, markets, and trends to assist businesses and investors in decision-making.
3. **Corporate Finance Manager**
    - **Role:** Financial Controller, Treasury Manager, CFO (Chief Financial Officer)

- Oversee financial planning, risk management, and budgeting for corporations.

4. **Investment Banker**
   - **Role:** Mergers & Acquisitions Advisor, Financial Consultant, Investment Banker
   - Assist companies in raising capital, structuring deals, and managing corporate financial strategies.
5. **Risk Manager**
   - **Role:** Credit Risk Manager, Operational Risk Analyst, Financial Risk Consultant
   - Assess and manage risks related to investments, loans, and financial products.
6. **Financial Planner**
   - **Role:** Personal Financial Advisor, Wealth Manager, Retirement Planning Consultant
   - Help individuals plan their finances, including investments, insurance, and retirement goals.
7. **Tax Consultant**
   - **Role:** Tax Planner, Tax Analyst, Tax Attorney

    - Advise individuals or businesses on tax-related matters and ensure compliance with tax laws.

8. **Management Consultant (Finance Focus)**
    - **Role:** Financial Strategy Consultant, Business Advisor
    - Provide businesses with financial strategies, operational efficiency, and investment planning.
9. **Investment Advisor**
    - **Role:** Financial Advisor, Wealth Manager
    - Guide clients on investment opportunities, portfolio management, and financial goals.
10. **Credit Analyst**
    - **Role:** Loan Officer, Credit Risk Analyst
    - Assess the creditworthiness of individuals or companies seeking loans or credit lines.
11. **Financial Auditor**
    - **Role:** Internal Auditor, Forensic Auditor
    - Conduct audits of financial statements and operations to ensure compliance and accuracy.

12. **Stockbroker**
    - **Role:** Trading Advisor, Equity Broker, Portfolio Manager
    - Buy and sell stocks on behalf of clients or firms, providing advice on market trends and investment opportunities.
13. **Actuary**
    - **Role:** Insurance Actuary, Risk Assessment Specialist
    - Use mathematical models to assess risk and uncertainty in financial products, particularly in insurance and pension schemes.
14. **Real Estate Finance Professional**
    - **Role:** Property Investment Analyst, Real Estate Fund Manager
    - Specialize in real estate investment, valuation, and financial strategies for the real estate market.
15. **Financial Data Analyst**
    - **Role:** Quantitative Analyst, Financial Researcher
    - Use data analysis techniques to interpret financial data, develop models, and predict market trends.

16. **Budget Analyst**
    - **Role:** Public Sector Budget Officer, Corporate Budget Manager
    - Prepare, analyze, and manage budgets for public agencies or private companies.
17. **Blockchain/FinTech Specialist**
    - **Role:** Blockchain Consultant, Cryptocurrency Analyst, FinTech Product Manager
    - Work in emerging financial technologies, specializing in cryptocurrency, blockchain, and digital finance systems.
18. **Compliance Officer**
    - **Role:** Financial Compliance Manager, Regulatory Compliance Officer
    - Ensure financial institutions comply with regulations, legal standards, and ethical practices.
19. **Hedge Fund Manager**
    - **Role:** Hedge Fund Analyst, Portfolio Manager
    - Manage hedge funds, make high-risk investments, and aim for substantial returns.

20. **FinTech Entrepreneur**
    - **Role:** Founder, Startup Financial Technology Advisor
    - Create or manage startups in the financial technology industry, focusing on innovation in financial products and services.

- ❖ Marketing

Career Pathway:

1. **Class 12th**: Commerce with focus on Marketing.
2. **UG**: BBA with Marketing specialization or B.Com in Marketing Management.
3. **PG**: MBA in Marketing or M.Com in Marketing Management.
4. **Professional Certifications**: Digital Marketing Certification, Google Ads Certification.

After studying **Commerce with Marketing**, here are some career options and roles you can enter:

1. **Marketing Manager**
    - **Role:** Oversee marketing strategies, campaigns, and teams to promote products or services and enhance brand visibility.

2. **Brand Manager**
    - **Role:** Manage and develop the brand identity, create brand strategies, and maintain consistency across marketing materials.
3. **Digital Marketing Specialist**
    - **Role:** Plan and execute digital marketing campaigns, including SEO, social media marketing, content marketing, and email marketing.
4. **Market Research Analyst**
    - **Role:** Conduct research to gather insights on consumer behavior, market trends, and competitor strategies, and provide actionable recommendations.
5. **Advertising Manager**
    - **Role:** Develop and manage advertising campaigns across various platforms, including TV, print, and digital media.
6. **Sales Manager**
    - **Role:** Lead a sales team, set sales targets, develop sales strategies, and manage client relationships to drive revenue.
7. **Public Relations (PR) Manager**
    - **Role:** Handle media relations, manage public perception, and create

communication strategies to promote a positive image for the company.

8. **Content Marketing Manager**
    - **Role:** Oversee content creation, strategy, and distribution to engage customers, build brand awareness, and drive traffic to websites.
9. **E-commerce Manager**
    - **Role:** Manage online sales platforms, create strategies to boost sales, and oversee digital marketing initiatives for e-commerce businesses.
10. **Product Manager**
    - **Role:** Guide product development, pricing, positioning, and lifecycle, ensuring products meet consumer needs and align with business goals.
11. **Social Media Manager**
    - **Role:** Manage social media accounts, create engaging content, and drive online community engagement to boost brand presence.
12. **Customer Relationship Manager (CRM)**
    - **Role:** Develop and manage customer relationships, implement CRM strategies, and ensure customer retention and satisfaction.

13. **Event Manager**
    - **Role:** Plan and execute events like product launches, trade shows, and corporate events to promote brands and create marketing opportunities.
14. **Retail Manager**
    - **Role:** Manage the operations of a retail store, develop sales strategies, and ensure a positive customer experience to drive retail success.
15. **Trade Marketing Manager**
    - **Role:** Create and implement marketing strategies for distribution channels, working closely with wholesalers, retailers, and sales teams.
16. **SEO/SEM Specialist**
    - **Role:** Optimize website content for search engines (SEO) and manage paid search campaigns (SEM) to increase web traffic and brand visibility.
17. **Affiliate Marketing Manager**
    - **Role:** Manage affiliate marketing programs, build relationships with affiliates, and track performance to drive sales through partnerships.

18. **Customer Insights Analyst**
    - **Role:** Analyze customer data and behavior to provide insights into product development, marketing strategies, and customer satisfaction.
19. **Campaign Manager**
    - **Role:** Plan and execute marketing campaigns across various channels (online and offline) to achieve brand and business objectives.
20. **Marketing Consultant**
    - **Role:** Provide expert advice to businesses on marketing strategies, consumer behavior, market positioning, and brand development.

❖ Entrepreneurship

Career Pathway:

1. **Class 12th**: Commerce with focus on Entrepreneurship.
2. **UG**: BBA or B.Com with Entrepreneurship specialization, **PG**: MBA in Entrepreneurship or M.Com in Entrepreneurship.
3. **Short Courses**: Startup Incubation Programs, Business Planning Courses

This Topic is Covered Separately In this book.

❖ Mathematics and Statistics

Career Pathway:

1. **Class 12th**: Commerce with Mathematics/Statistics.
2. **UG**: B.Sc. in Mathematics or Statistics, Bachelor of Management Studies (BMS), Bachelor of Business Administration (BBA)
3. **PG**: M.Sc. in Applied Mathematics, Statistics, or Actuarial Science.
4. **Professional Certifications**: Actuarial Science Certifications, Data Science Programs.

After studying Commerce with Mathematics and Statistics, here are some career options and roles you can enter:

Data Analyst

- **Role:** Analyze data to uncover trends, patterns, and insights to support business decisions, using statistical tools and software.

Financial Analyst

- **Role:** Analyze financial data, markets, and trends to help businesses make informed financial decisions, including forecasting and budgeting.

Actuary

- **Role:** Assess and manage risk using mathematical and statistical methods, especially in insurance, pension planning, and investment.

Business Analyst

- **Role:** Analyze business processes and data to identify opportunities for improvement, supporting strategic decision-making.

Operations Research Analyst

- **Role:** Apply mathematical and statistical methods to solve business problems, optimize processes, and improve decision-making in industries like logistics and manufacturing.

Statistician

- **Role:** Use statistical techniques to collect, analyze, and interpret data for various applications, such as market research, healthcare, and government projects.

Market Research Analyst

- **Role:** Collect and analyze data on consumer behavior, market conditions, and trends to help companies make informed marketing and business decisions.

Risk Manager

- **Role:** Identify, assess, and manage financial and operational risks, often in fields such as banking, insurance, and investment.

Economist

- **Role:** Use statistical and mathematical methods to analyze economic data, model economic trends, and assist in policy-making or business strategy.

Investment Analyst

- **Role:** Analyze financial markets and investment opportunities using mathematical models and statistical analysis to recommend investments.

Quantitative Analyst (Quant)

- **Role:** Develop and implement complex mathematical models to analyze financial data, often in investment banking, hedge funds, or trading firms.

Supply Chain Analyst

- **Role:** Use data analysis and mathematical modeling to optimize supply chain operations, including inventory management, distribution, and logistics.

Data Scientist

- **Role:** Use advanced statistical and machine learning techniques to analyze large datasets, build predictive models, and drive business insights.

Portfolio Manager

- **Role:** Manage investment portfolios, using statistical tools to assess risk and return and optimize asset allocation.

Operations Manager

- **Role:** Oversee and improve business operations, applying quantitative analysis and statistical tools to optimize efficiency and productivity.

Credit Analyst

- **Role:** Assess the creditworthiness of individuals or businesses, using financial data, statistical methods, and credit models.

Health Economist

- **Role:** Apply statistical and mathematical models to healthcare data to assess costs, outcomes, and efficiency in healthcare systems and policies.

Financial Planner

- **Role:** Use mathematical and statistical tools to advise individuals on managing their finances, investments, and retirement planning.

Supply Chain Optimization Analyst

- **Role:** Use mathematical models and statistical analysis to improve supply chain efficiency, reducing costs and enhancing logistics.

Consultant (Data/Analytics)

- **Role:** Provide expert advice on data-driven decision-making and analytics, helping organizations optimize their business strategies with mathematical and statistical insights.

Legal Studies

Career Pathway:

1. **Class 12th**: Commerce with Legal Studies.
2. **UG**: Integrated BBA LLB or B.Com LLB.
3. **PG**: Master of Laws (LLM) in Business or Corporate Law.
4. **Professional Certifications**: Company Secretary (CS), Legal Compliance Certifications. Corporate Governance

After studying Commerce with Legal Studies, here are some career options and roles you can enter:

Corporate Lawyer

- **Role:** Provide legal advice to businesses on a range of matters such as mergers, acquisitions, intellectual property, contracts, and compliance.

Legal Advisor

- **Role:** Offer legal counsel and guidance to individuals or organizations on matters like contracts, labor law, tax law, and regulatory issues.

Compliance Officer

- **Role:** Ensure that businesses comply with regulatory and legal requirements, mitigating risks and maintaining ethical standards.

Corporate Legal Counsel

- **Role:** Represent the company in legal matters, draft and review contracts, ensure legal compliance, and manage legal risks.

Intellectual Property (IP) Consultant

- **Role:** Advise companies on protecting their intellectual property rights, including patents, trademarks, copyrights, and trade secrets.

Contracts Manager

- **Role:** Oversee the drafting, negotiation, and enforcement of contracts between businesses, clients, and partners.

Legal Manager

- **Role:** Manage and oversee a company's legal affairs, ensuring legal compliance and advising on business-related legal matters.

Tax Consultant

- **Role:** Provide advice on tax-related issues, including tax planning, compliance, and strategy, often for businesses or high-net-worth individuals.

Litigation Support Specialist

- **Role:** Provide legal research and case support for lawyers and legal teams, preparing documents, managing case files, and assisting in trial preparation.

Company Secretary

- **Role:** Oversee corporate governance, ensure compliance with company law, manage regulatory filings, and advise the board of directors on legal matters.

Arbitrator

- **Role:** Act as a neutral third party to resolve disputes outside the court system, often in commercial, contractual, or labor-related issues.

Legal Researcher

- **Role:** Conduct legal research to assist law firms, businesses, or government agencies in interpreting laws, regulations, and case precedents.

Labor Law Consultant

- **Role:** Advise organizations on labor laws, employee rights, industrial relations, and compliance with employment-related regulations.

Insurance Claim Adjuster

- **Role:** Assess and manage insurance claims, ensuring they meet legal requirements and company policies, often dealing with business-related claims.

Real Estate Lawyer

- **Role:** Provide legal services related to property law, including property transactions, leases, disputes, and zoning regulations.

Regulatory Affairs Specialist

- **Role:** Ensure that a business adheres to governmental regulations and industry standards, particularly in sectors like pharmaceuticals, finance, or energy.

Banking and Finance Lawyer

- **Role:** Specialize in legal issues surrounding the financial industry, including securities, investments, loans, and banking regulations.

Financial Services Lawyer

- **Role:** Offer legal services to businesses in the financial services sector, advising on compliance, regulations, mergers, acquisitions, and finance-related disputes.

Cybersecurity Legal Consultant

- **Role:** Provide legal advice on data protection, privacy laws, cybersecurity regulations, and compliance with data security laws.

Environmental Law Consultant

- **Role:** Advise businesses on environmental regulations, sustainability practices, and compliance with environmental protection laws.

❖ Information Technology in Business

Career Pathway:

1. **Class 12th**: Commerce with IT as an elective.
2. **UG**: B.Tech in IT or BBA in IT Management.
3. **PG**: MBA in IT or M.Sc. in Information Systems.
4. **Professional Certifications**: Data Analytics, Cybersecurity Certification

An MBA in IT equips you with both business acumen and technical expertise, allowing you to pursue leadership roles in IT management, digital transformation, and technology strategy across various industries.

Various Roles on can manage along with IT with Commerce and IT combination are:

IT Project Manager

- **Role:** Lead and manage IT projects, ensuring successful delivery, optimal resource allocation, and alignment with business goals.

Chief Information Officer (CIO)

- **Role:** Oversee the technology strategy for an organization, ensuring that IT investments align with business objectives and drive innovation.

IT Consultant

- **Role:** Provide expert advice to organizations on how to leverage IT solutions to improve business processes, enhance efficiency, and reduce costs.

Business Intelligence (BI) Manager

- **Role:** Lead teams that analyze business data and provide actionable insights using data analytics and business intelligence tools to support strategic decisions.

E-commerce Manager

- **Role:** Manage and optimize online sales platforms, including digital marketing, user experience design, and sales strategy development.

Technology Strategist

- **Role:** Develop and implement technology strategies that help businesses stay competitive, optimize operations, and achieve growth.

Enterprise Resource Planning (ERP) Manager

- **Role:** Manage the implementation, optimization, and support of ERP systems, ensuring they meet the company's business and operational needs.

Digital Transformation Manager

- **Role:** Drive digital initiatives across organizations, helping businesses transition from traditional models to more technology-driven, automated solutions.

IT Operations Manager

- **Role:** Oversee the day-to-day operations of IT systems, ensuring that hardware, software, and networks run efficiently and securely.

Cybersecurity Manager

- **Role:** Lead cybersecurity efforts within an organization, ensuring the protection of critical data and IT infrastructure from cyber threats and breaches.

Data Analytics Manager

- **Role:** Oversee teams responsible for gathering, analyzing, and interpreting data to make data-driven decisions and strategies for the business.

Cloud Solutions Architect

- **Role:** Design and manage cloud computing systems, helping businesses migrate to cloud platforms and optimize their infrastructure.

IT Risk Manager

- **Role:** Identify, assess, and mitigate risks related to IT infrastructure, data security, and compliance.

IT Governance Manager

- **Role:** Ensure that IT policies and procedures align with business goals, regulatory requirements, and industry standards.

Mobile Application Manager

- **Role:** Manage the development and maintenance of mobile applications, focusing on performance, security, and usability.

AI/ML Manager

- **Role:** Lead initiatives involving artificial intelligence (AI) and machine learning (ML), integrating these technologies into business processes to drive efficiency and innovation.

Blockchain Consultant

- **Role:** Advise companies on the integration of blockchain technology into business operations, enhancing security and transparency.

Technology Integration Manager

- **Role:** Manage the integration of new IT systems and software into existing business processes, ensuring minimal disruption and maximizing value.

CRM Manager (Customer Relationship Management)

- **Role:** Oversee the implementation and management of CRM systems, focusing on customer data analytics and improving customer experiences.

Digital Marketing Manager

- ❖ **Role:** Manage online marketing campaigns, social media strategies, and digital presence, leveraging IT tools to reach and engage customers effectively.
- ❖ Human Resource Management

Career Pathway:

1. **Class 12th**: Commerce with focus on HR.
2. **UG**: BBA with HR specialization or B.Com in Human Resource Development.
3. **PG**: MBA in Human Resource Management or Master of Human Resource Management (MHRM).
4. **Professional Certifications**: SHRM Certified Professional, HR Analytics Certification

After studying Commerce with a focus on **Human Resource Management (HR)**, here are some career options and roles you can pursue:

- ❖ **HR Manager**
  - ➢ Role: Oversee and manage HR functions such as recruitment, employee relations, performance management, and training and development.

- **Talent Acquisition Specialist**
  - Role: Handle the recruitment process, identifying and attracting top talent for various positions within the organization.
- **HR Consultant**
  - Role: Provide expert advice and guidance to organizations on HR practices, policies, and strategies to improve employee engagement, performance, and retention.
- **Employee Relations Manager**
  - Role: Manage the relationship between employees and employers, addressing concerns, resolving conflicts, and ensuring a positive work environment.
- **Compensation and Benefits Manager**
  - Role: Design and manage compensation packages, benefits programs, and performance-related bonuses to ensure competitiveness and employee satisfaction.
- **Training and Development Manager**
  - Role: Plan, implement, and manage training programs to improve employees' skills, performance, and career development.

- **HR Business Partner**
    - Role: Work closely with business leaders to align HR strategies with organizational goals and drive employee engagement and performance.
- **Payroll Manager**
    - Role: Manage the payroll process, ensuring timely and accurate processing of employee salaries, benefits, and deductions.
- **HR Data Analyst**
    - Role: Analyze HR data, using analytics to drive decisions related to employee performance, retention, and HR operations.
- **Recruitment Manager**
    - Role: Oversee the entire recruitment process, managing recruitment teams, sourcing candidates, and developing effective hiring strategies.
- **Organizational Development Manager**
    - Role: Focus on improving organizational efficiency, culture, and structure through strategic planning, change management, and employee development.

- **HR Information Systems (HRIS) Manager**
  - Role: Manage HR-related software systems and technology platforms that streamline HR operations such as recruitment, payroll, and employee data management.
- **Workforce Planning Manager**
  - Role: Plan and manage staffing levels, ensuring that the organization has the right people in the right roles at the right time.
- **Diversity and Inclusion Manager**
  - Role: Develop and implement programs that promote diversity, equity, and inclusion within the workplace.
- **Industrial Relations Manager**
  - Role: Manage relationships between management and labor unions, ensuring compliance with labor laws and handling collective bargaining issues.
- **Learning and Development Specialist**
  - Role: Focus on developing and implementing learning strategies to enhance employees' professional skills and personal growth.

- **HR Generalist**
    - Role: Handle a wide range of HR functions, including recruitment, onboarding, employee relations, and performance management.
- **Change Management Specialist**
    - Role: Lead organizational change initiatives, helping employees and leaders adapt to changes in processes, systems, or organizational structure.
- **HR Director**
    - Role: Oversee the overall HR strategy and policies of an organization, ensuring alignment with business goals and fostering a positive workplace culture.
- **Health and Safety Officer**
    - Role: Ensure compliance with occupational health and safety regulations, and manage programs aimed at protecting employees' well-being.
- Ethics and Corporate Governance

Career Pathway:

1. **Class 12th**: Commerce with focus on Business Ethics.

2. **UG**: BBA or B.Com with Corporate Governance as an elective.
3. **PG**: MBA in Corporate Governance or specialized certifications like Certified Compliance and Ethics Professional (CCEP).

After studying **Ethics and Corporate Governance** within the **Commerce stream**, here are some career options and roles you can pursue:

- **Corporate Governance Manager**
  - Role: Ensure that the organization adheres to governance standards, policies, and best practices, while promoting transparency, accountability, and ethical behavior.
- **Compliance Officer**
  - Role: Ensure that a company complies with laws, regulations, and internal policies. Often works in industries like finance, healthcare, and manufacturing.
- **Ethics Officer**
  - Role: Develop and oversee ethical policies and practices within an organization, ensuring that ethical standards are met in business operations.

- **Corporate Social Responsibility (CSR) Manager**
  - Role: Lead and manage corporate social responsibility initiatives, ensuring that the company's activities align with ethical standards and contribute positively to society.
- **Internal Auditor**
  - Role: Evaluate and improve the effectiveness of internal controls, risk management, and governance processes, ensuring compliance with laws and ethical standards.
- **Risk Manager**
  - Role: Identify, assess, and manage organizational risks, focusing on governance, compliance, and ethical risk factors.
- **Sustainability Manager**
  - Role: Develop and manage sustainability strategies, ensuring the organization's operations are environmentally responsible and socially ethical.
- **Legal and Compliance Consultant**
  - Role: Advise businesses on legal matters related to governance,

compliance, and ethical practices, ensuring they meet all regulatory requirements.

- ❖ **Corporate Governance Consultant**
  - ➢ Role: Provide consulting services to organizations on improving governance structures, policies, and practices to ensure transparency and ethical decision-making.
- ❖ **Ethical Investment Analyst**
  - ➢ Role: Analyze investment opportunities based on ethical criteria, advising investors on socially responsible and ethically sound investment options.
- ❖ **Governance Risk and Compliance (GRC) Analyst**
  - ➢ Role: Focus on assessing and managing an organization's risk management, governance, and compliance practices, often using specialized software and tools.
- ❖ **Company Secretary**
  - ➢ Role: Ensure corporate governance is maintained in the organization, including compliance with statutory and regulatory requirements, and reporting to the board of directors.

- ❖ **Board Advisor**
  - ➢ Role: Provide advice to company boards on governance best practices, ethical decision-making, and corporate responsibility.
- ❖ **Legal Compliance Officer**
  - ➢ Role: Oversee legal compliance in business operations, ensuring the organization's activities align with legal, regulatory, and ethical standards.
- ❖ **Business Ethics Consultant**
  - ➢ Role: Advise organizations on ethical challenges in business practices and help develop strategies to address them effectively.
- ❖ **Human Rights Officer**
  - ➢ Role: Oversee compliance with human rights standards within an organization, particularly in industries or regions where human rights may be at risk.
- ❖ **Governance and Accountability Specialist**
  - ➢ Role: Ensure that organizations are accountable for their actions, particularly in the public and non-profit sectors, focusing on ethical governance practices.

- **Corporate Ethics and Compliance Auditor**
    - Role: Conduct audits to assess whether an organization adheres to ethical guidelines, legal regulations, and corporate policies.
- **Financial Compliance Manager**
    - Role: Ensure that the company complies with financial regulations and standards, focusing on the ethical handling of financial transactions.
- **Whistleblowing Officer**
    - Role: Manage and address concerns raised by employees about unethical or illegal activities within an organization, providing a safe environment for whistleblowers.
- International Business

Career Pathway:

1. **Class 12th**: Commerce with International Trade focus.
2. **UG**: BBA with International Business specialization or B.Com in International Trade.
3. **PG**: MBA in International Business or M.Com in International Business.
4. **Professional Certifications**: Export-Import Management Certification, International Trade Certification.

After studying **International Business**, here are some career options and roles you can pursue:

1. **International Business Manager**
   - Role: Oversee global business operations, develop strategies for international markets, and manage cross-border teams.
2. **Export Manager**
   - Role: Manage the export process for goods and services, identifying international market opportunities and ensuring compliance with global trade regulations.
3. **Global Supply Chain Manager**
   - Role: Coordinate international supply chains, optimizing sourcing, manufacturing, and distribution across multiple countries.
4. **International Marketing Manager**
   - Role: Develop and implement marketing strategies for international markets, focusing on adapting products and campaigns to local cultures and preferences.
5. **International Trade Consultant**
   - Role: Advise businesses on international trade laws, tariffs, market

entry strategies, and logistics to expand into new global markets.

6. **Foreign Affairs Specialist**
   - Role: Manage relationships between governments, organizations, and international institutions, often working with diplomats, trade representatives, and policy makers.
7. **Global Financial Analyst**
   - Role: Analyze global financial markets, economic trends, and investment opportunities for international corporations and investors.
8. **International Business Development Manager**
   - Role: Identify and develop new international business opportunities, focusing on building relationships with foreign markets and partners.
9. **Cross-Cultural Consultant**
   - Role: Advise organizations on how to effectively operate in different cultural environments, ensuring successful market entry and management in international settings.

10. **Import/Export Coordinator**
    - Role: Oversee the logistics of importing and exporting goods between countries, ensuring compliance with international trade regulations and minimizing operational costs.
11. **International Sales Manager**
    - Role: Manage sales teams focused on international markets, developing strategies to increase sales and expand global customer bases.
12. **Foreign Exchange Trader**
    - Role: Engage in trading currencies on the foreign exchange market, using knowledge of global markets to predict exchange rate movements.
13. **International Human Resources Manager**
    - Role: Manage recruitment, training, and compliance across multiple countries, handling global staffing and cross-border employment issues.
14. **Global Account Manager**
    - Role: Manage relationships with large international clients, ensuring their needs are met across different countries and regions.

15. **International Logistics Manager**
    - Role: Coordinate the movement of goods and services internationally, optimizing transportation, customs, and warehousing processes.
16. **Trade Compliance Officer**
    - Role: Ensure compliance with international trade laws, regulations, and tariffs for businesses engaged in cross-border transactions.
17. **International Project Manager**
    - Role: Manage international projects across different countries, ensuring timely execution, budget management, and cross-cultural collaboration.
18. **Global Risk Manager**
    - Role: Identify and mitigate risks associated with operating in international markets, including political, economic, and legal risks.
19. **Global Brand Manager**
    - Role: Oversee the development and management of a brand's global presence, ensuring consistent messaging and product adaptation across diverse markets.

20. **International Relations Manager**
    - Role: Build and maintain relationships with foreign governments, international businesses, and NGOs to foster strategic partnerships and collaborations.

Below is the comprehensive list of Degrees and Diploma in Commerce Files one can purse.

Here is a comprehensive list of **Diploma and Degree** options under the **Commerce** field:

Diploma Courses in Commerce

1. **Diploma in Accounting**
2. **Diploma in Business Administration**
3. **Diploma in Financial Accounting**
4. **Diploma in Business Management**
5. **Diploma in Taxation**
6. **Diploma in International Business**
7. **Diploma in Digital Marketing**
8. **Diploma in Human Resource Management**
9. **Diploma in Export and Import Management**
10. **Diploma in Banking and Finance**
11. **Diploma in Retail Management**
12. **Diploma in Entrepreneurship**
13. **Diploma in Supply Chain Management**
14. **Diploma in Financial Planning**

15. **Diploma in Insurance**
16. **Diploma in E-Commerce**
17. **Diploma in Company Secretaryship**
18. **Diploma in Marketing Management**
19. **Diploma in Logistics and Supply Chain Management**
20. **Diploma in Event Management**

Degree Courses in Commerce

1. **Bachelor of Commerce (B.Com)**
    - General
    - Honors
    - Specialization options (e.g., Accounting, Finance, Marketing)
2. **Bachelor of Business Administration (BBA)**
    - General
    - Specializations like Marketing, HR, Finance, IT, International Business
3. **Bachelor of Management Studies (BMS)**
4. **Bachelor of Economics (B.A. or B.Sc.)**
5. **Bachelor of Finance and Accounting (BFA)**
6. **Bachelor of Computer Applications (BCA)**
7. **Bachelor of Business Administration in International Business (BBA-IB)**

8. **Bachelor of Commerce (B.Com) in Computer Applications**
9. **Bachelor of Business Administration in Hospitality Management**
10. **Bachelor of Hotel Management (BHM)**
11. **Bachelor of Retail Management**
12. **Bachelor of Tourism Management (BTTM)**
13. **Bachelor of Event Management**
14. **Bachelor of Marketing Management**
15. **Bachelor of Supply Chain Management**

Postgraduate Degree Courses

1. **Master of Commerce (M.Com)**
    - Specializations (Accounting, Finance, Banking, International Business)
2. **Master of Business Administration (MBA)**
    - Specializations (Marketing, Finance, HR, Operations, International Business, Entrepreneurship)
3. **Master of Business Administration in International Business (MBA-IB)**
4. **Master of Business Administration in Finance (MBA-Finance)**
5. **Master of Business Administration in Marketing (MBA-Marketing)**
6. **Master of Financial Management (MFM)**

7. **Master of Economics (M.A./M.Sc. Economics)**
8. **Master of Business Law (MBL)**
9. **Master of Human Resource Management (MHRM)**
10. **Master of International Business (MIB)**
11. **Master of Supply Chain Management (MSCM)**
12. **Master of Marketing Management (MMM)**

Professional Courses

1. **Chartered Accountancy (CA)**
2. **Company Secretary (CS)**
3. **Cost and Management Accountancy (CMA)**
4. **Certified Financial Planner (CFP)**
5. **Financial Risk Manager (FRM)**
6. **Certified Management Accountant (CMA)**
7. **Certified Internal Auditor (CIA)**
8. **Certified Public Accountant (CPA)**
9. **Chartered Financial Analyst (CFA)**
10. **Digital Marketing Certification**

Here is a list of common **entrance exams** for students pursuing courses in the **Commerce stream**:

Undergraduate Entrance Exams (For B.Com, BBA, BMS, etc.):

1. **Common Entrance Test (CET)** – Conducted by various state universities for admission into BBA, B.Com, and related courses.
2. **DU JAT (Delhi University Joint Admission Test)** – For admission to BBA, BMS, and related undergraduate courses at Delhi University.
3. **NPAT (NMIMS Programs After Twelfth)** – Conducted by NMIMS for admission to BBA, B.Com, and related courses.
4. **IPU CET (Indraprastha University Common Entrance Test)** – For admission to BBA, BCA, and B.Com courses in IP University, Delhi.
5. **SET (Symbiosis Entrance Test)** – For admission to undergraduate courses like BBA, B.Com, and other related courses at Symbiosis University.
6. **AIMA UGAT (Under Graduate Aptitude Test)** – For admission to BBA and related undergraduate programs.
7. **CET (Common Entrance Test)** – Conducted by various private universities like Christ University, for admission to BBA, B.Com, and other commerce-related courses.
8. **MAH CET (Maharashtra Common Entrance Test)** – For admission to BBA, BCA, and B.Com programs in Maharashtra.

9. **St. Xavier's College Entrance Exam** - For admission to BMS, BBA, and other undergraduate courses in Mumbai.
10. **BBA/BMS Entrance Exams (Various Universities)** - Each university like Pune University, Bangalore University, etc., conducts their own entrance exams for BBA and BMS admissions.

Postgraduate Entrance Exams (For MBA, M.Com, etc.):

1. **CAT (Common Admission Test)** - For admission to MBA/PGDM programs in top IIMs and other business schools.
2. **XAT (Xavier Aptitude Test)** – For admission to MBA/PGDM programs in Xavier Institute and other institutes.
3. **MAT (Management Aptitude Test)** - For admission to MBA/PGDM programs in various business schools across India.
4. **CMAT (Common Management Admission Test)** - For admission to MBA/PGDM programs in AICTE-approved institutes.
5. **SNAP (Symbiosis National Aptitude Test)** - For admission to MBA programs in Symbiosis Institute of Business Management (SIBM) and other Symbiosis institutes.
6. **NMAT (NMIMS Management Aptitude Test)** – For admission to MBA programs in NMIMS.

7. **IBSAT (ICFAI Business Studies Aptitude Test)** - For admission to MBA programs at ICFAI Business Schools.
8. **TISSNET (Tata Institute of Social Sciences National Entrance Test)** - For admission to various social science programs, including HR and business courses.
9. **IIFT (Indian Institute of Foreign Trade)** - For admission to MBA (International Business) programs.
10. **MICA (Mudra Institute of Communications Ahmedabad) Entrance Exam** - For admission to MBA (Communication) programs.
11. **PGDBM (Post Graduate Diploma in Business Management) Entrance Exams** - Various business schools conduct their own exams for PGDBM courses.

Professional Certification Entrance Exams:

1. **CA Foundation (Chartered Accountancy) Exam** - For admission to the CA course (after Class 12).
2. **CMA Foundation (Cost Management Accounting) Exam** - For admission to the CMA course.
3. **CS Foundation (Company Secretary) Exam** - For admission to the CS course.

4. **CFA (Chartered Financial Analyst) Exam** – For admission to the CFA course, which requires passing Level I, II, and III.
5. **FRM (Financial Risk Manager) Exam** – For certification in financial risk management.
6. **CFP (Certified Financial Planner) Exam** – For certification in financial planning.

Specialized Commerce and Business Exams:

1. **CLAT (Common Law Admission Test)** – For admission to law programs (includes commercial law and business law).
2. **NCHM JEE (National Council for Hotel Management Joint Entrance Exam)** – For admission to BHM programs, which can be pursued under the commerce stream.
3. **IIM-IPM (Integrated Program in Management)** – For admission to a 5-year integrated MBA program for students after Class 12.
4. **BBA/BMS Entrance Exams (various universities)** – Includes specific exams for institutions offering BBA or BMS programs.

These entrance exams provide pathways for commerce students to enter prestigious undergraduate, postgraduate, or professional programs in commerce, business, management, economics, law, and related fields.

Science:

One of the most popular academic pathways for students after grade 10 is the science stream, especially for those who want to work in technology, engineering, research, medicine, and other scientific fields. Depending on their chosen specialization, students in the science stream usually study subjects like mathematics, physics, chemistry, and biology.

There are two main branches of the stream:

- Medical: Serves students interested in careers in medicine, healthcare, pharmacy, biotechnology, and related fields by emphasizing courses like biology, chemistry, and physics.
- Non-Medical: Contains courses like mathematics, physics, and chemistry that are perfect for students who want to study computer science, engineering, architecture, and other technical fields.

The science stream provides a variety of career options and fosters analytical, critical thinking, and problem-solving abilities.

Some of the Very Known Career Options in Science Stream are below:

1. Medical Stream (Biology, Chemistry, Physics)

The medical stream is for students interested in healthcare, life sciences, and medical professions. It combines Biology, Chemistry, and Physics, with a focus on human health and wellness.

Subject Group for Medical Stream:

- **Subjects**: Biology, Chemistry, Physics (optional)

Career Options in the Medical Stream:

- **Doctor (MBBS)**: Diagnose and treat diseases, promote overall health.
- **Dentist (BDS)**: Specialize in oral health, including teeth, gums, and mouth.
- **Pharmacist**: Focus on the preparation and dispensing of medications.
- **Nurse**: Work in healthcare settings, assisting doctors and patients.
- **Biotechnologist**: Apply biological principles to develop technologies in healthcare, agriculture, and environmental science.
- **Physiotherapist**: Help patients recover movement and function after injuries.
- **Lab Technician**: Conduct tests and experiments in labs to support medical diagnoses.
- **Optometrist**: Focus on eye care and vision correction.
- **Veterinarian**: Treat animals and diagnose their illnesses.

- **Biochemist**: Study chemical processes within living organisms.
- **Genetic Counselor**: Advise individuals on genetic disorders and inheritance patterns.
- **Health Administrator**: Manage healthcare facilities, ensuring efficient operations.
- **Radiologist**: Specialize in interpreting medical images, such as X-rays and MRIs.

2. Non-Medical Stream (Physics, Chemistry, Mathematics)

The non-medical stream focuses on subjects like Physics, Chemistry, and Mathematics, and is perfect for students pursuing engineering, technology, and various technical professions.

Subject Group for Non-Medical Stream:

- **Subjects**: Physics, Chemistry, Mathematics (optional)

Career Options in the Non-Medical Stream:

- **Engineer**: Work in various disciplines such as Mechanical, Civil, Electrical, Computer Science, and Aerospace Engineering.
- **Architect**: Design buildings and structures, ensuring functionality, safety, and aesthetics.
- **Computer Scientist**: Focus on the development of software, hardware, and systems.

- **Mathematician**: Apply mathematical principles to solve real-world problems in various fields like finance, engineering, and technology.
- **Data Scientist**: Analyze and interpret complex data to help organizations make decisions.
- **Physicist**: Study the fundamental properties of matter, energy, and the universe.
- **Astronomer**: Study celestial bodies and the universe beyond Earth.
- **Chemist**: Work in chemical industries, research, and development.
- **Pilot**: Operate aircraft for commercial, private, or military purposes.
- **Civil Services**: Work in government administration in various departments (with additional preparation).
- **Robotics Engineer**: Design and develop robots and automated systems.
- **IT Consultant**: Advise organizations on technology and IT solutions.
- **Cybersecurity Expert**: Protect digital systems and networks from cyber threats.

New-age careers in science are emerging fields driven by advancements in technology, innovation, and a deeper understanding of science. These careers often blend traditional scientific knowledge with cutting-edge technologies and interdisciplinary approaches. Below are some of the most promising new-age science careers:

1. Artificial Intelligence (AI) and Machine Learning Specialist

- **Role**: Develop algorithms, models, and systems that allow machines to learn from data and make decisions.
- **Skills**: Strong knowledge of programming languages (Python, R), machine learning algorithms, data analysis, and statistics.
- **Industries**: Technology, healthcare, finance, and robotics.

2. Data Scientist

- **Role**: Analyze large sets of data to extract useful insights, make predictions, and help businesses make data-driven decisions.
- **Skills**: Statistical analysis, machine learning, programming (Python, SQL), data visualization tools.
- **Industries**: Finance, healthcare, e-commerce, marketing, and research.

3. Genomics and Biotechnology Specialist

- **Role**: Work on genetic research, gene editing (like CRISPR), and biotechnology applications for medicine, agriculture, and environmental sustainability.

- **Skills**: Molecular biology, genetic engineering, biotechnology tools, bioinformatics.
- **Industries**: Pharmaceuticals, healthcare, agriculture, and environmental science.

4. Robotics Engineer

- **Role**: Design, develop, and maintain robots that can perform a variety of tasks autonomously or assist humans in industries like manufacturing, healthcare, and space exploration.
- **Skills**: Mechanical engineering, electrical engineering, computer programming, artificial intelligence.
- **Industries**: Manufacturing, healthcare, space, defense, and research.

5. Cybersecurity Expert (in Scientific Fields)

- **Role**: Protect sensitive scientific data, research, and technological infrastructures from cyberattacks and unauthorized access.
- **Skills**: Knowledge of cryptography, ethical hacking, network security, and cybersecurity protocols.
- **Industries**: Information technology, government agencies, healthcare, and scientific research organizations.

6. Environmental Scientist (with a focus on Climate Change)

- **Role**: Study and develop solutions for climate change, sustainable energy, and conservation efforts using advanced scientific techniques.
- **Skills**: Environmental science, renewable energy technologies, data analysis, climate modeling.
- **Industries**: Government, non-profits, energy sector, and research institutions.

7. Nanotechnology Engineer

- **Role**: Work with materials at the nanometer scale to create new products with applications in medicine, electronics, and materials science.
- **Skills**: Knowledge of nanomaterials, chemistry, engineering, and physics.
- **Industries**: Healthcare, electronics, energy, and material science.

8. Quantum Computing Specialist

- **Role**: Work with quantum mechanics to develop computers and algorithms that are exponentially faster than classical computers.
- **Skills**: Quantum physics, computer science, mathematics, programming (Python, C++).
- **Industries**: Technology, cryptography, pharmaceuticals, and finance.

9. Space Scientist / Astrobiologist

- **Role**: Study the possibility of life beyond Earth and conduct research related to space exploration and colonization.
- **Skills**: Astrobiology, physics, astronomy, and data science.
- **Industries**: Space agencies, research institutions, and private space exploration companies.

10. Virtual Reality (VR) / Augmented Reality (AR) Developer (in Healthcare and Education)

- **Role**: Develop immersive VR/AR experiences for medical training, education, or therapeutic purposes.
- **Skills**: 3D modeling, computer programming (Unity, C#), and understanding of human psychology and sensory systems.
- **Industries**: Healthcare, education, gaming, and entertainment.

11. Bioinformatics Specialist

- **Role**: Use computational tools to analyze biological data, especially in genomics, and provide insights into diseases and treatments.
- **Skills**: Data analysis, programming (Python, R), and biology.
- **Industries**: Pharmaceuticals, healthcare, and research institutions.

12. Sustainability Scientist (Green Tech)

- **Role**: Research and develop new technologies or processes to reduce environmental impact and promote sustainable practices.
- **Skills**: Environmental science, engineering, renewable energy, and sustainability practices.
- **Industries**: Energy, manufacturing, environmental agencies, and research.

13. Neuroscientist (with a focus on AI Integration)

- **Role**: Study the brain and nervous system, particularly in relation to AI, neuroprosthetics, and brain-computer interfaces.
- **Skills**: Neuroscience, computational modeling, machine learning, and neurotechnology.
- **Industries**: Healthcare, technology, research, and pharmaceuticals.

14. Personalized Medicine Specialist

- **Role**: Use genomic and clinical data to provide tailored medical treatments for patients.
- **Skills**: Genetics, bioinformatics, clinical data analysis.
- **Industries**: Healthcare, pharmaceuticals, and biotechnology.

15. 3D Printing Specialist (in Medicine and Engineering)

- **Role**: Design and develop 3D-printed organs, prosthetics, or complex engineering solutions.
- **Skills**: 3D printing technologies, design software, materials science.
- **Industries**: Healthcare, manufacturing, aerospace, and automotive.

Degree Courses in Science Stream

1. Bachelor of Science (B.Sc.)

- **General B.Sc.**: A broad degree with subjects like Physics, Chemistry, Biology, Mathematics, etc.
- **Specialized B.Sc.**: Focus on specific subjects, such as:
    - **B.Sc. in Physics**
    - **B.Sc. in Chemistry**
    - **B.Sc. in Biology**
    - **B.Sc. in Mathematics**
    - **B.Sc. in Environmental Science**
    - **B.Sc. in Biotechnology**
    - **B.Sc. in Microbiology**
    - **B.Sc. in Botany**
    - **B.Sc. in Zoology**
    - **B.Sc. in Biochemistry**
    - **B.Sc. in Genetics**

2. Bachelor of Technology (B.Tech) / Bachelor of Engineering (B.E.)

- **B.Tech in Computer Science**
- **B.Tech in Mechanical Engineering**
- **B.Tech in Civil Engineering**
- **B.Tech in Electrical Engineering**
- **B.Tech in Chemical Engineering**
- **B.Tech in Electronics and Communication Engineering**
- **B.Tech in Aerospace Engineering**
- **B.Tech in Biotechnology**
- **B.Tech in Artificial Intelligence**
- **B.Tech in Robotics**
- **B.Tech in Environmental Engineering**

3. Medical Degrees

- **Bachelor of Medicine, Bachelor of Surgery (MBBS)**: For aspiring doctors.
- **Bachelor of Dental Surgery (BDS)**: For aspiring dentists.
- **Bachelor of Pharmacy (B.Pharm)**: For pharmacy professionals.
- **B.Sc. Nursing**: For aspiring nurses.
- **B.V.Sc. (Bachelor of Veterinary Science)**: For veterinary professionals.

4. Bachelor's in Applied Sciences

- **B.Sc. in Forensic Science**
- **B.Sc. in Food Technology**
- **B.Sc. in Fashion Technology**
- **B.Sc. in Home Science**
- **B.Sc. in Hospitality and Hotel Administration**

5. Bachelor's in Computational Sciences

- **B.Sc. in Computer Science**
- **B.Sc. in Information Technology**
- **B.Sc. in Data Science**
- **B.Sc. in Cyber Security**

6. Bachelor of Science in Agriculture

- For students interested in agriculture, farming technologies, and rural development.

7. Bachelor of Science in Environmental Science

- Focuses on studying environmental issues, conservation, and sustainability.

Diploma Courses in Science Stream

1. Diploma in Engineering/Technology

- **Diploma in Mechanical Engineering**
- **Diploma in Civil Engineering**
- **Diploma in Electrical Engineering**
- **Diploma in Electronics Engineering**

- **Diploma in Computer Science Engineering**
- **Diploma in Chemical Engineering**
- **Diploma in Biotechnology**
- **Diploma in Aeronautical Engineering**
- **Diploma in Environmental Engineering**

2. Diploma in Medical Sciences

- **Diploma in Nursing (GNM)**: General Nursing and Midwifery.
- **Diploma in Pharmacy (D.Pharm)**: For those pursuing a career in pharmacy.
- **Diploma in Medical Laboratory Technology**: For laboratory technicians.
- **Diploma in Radiology and Imaging Technology**: For radiology technicians.
- **Diploma in Physiotherapy**: For physiotherapists.
- **Diploma in Optometry**: For eye care professionals.

3. Diploma in Applied Sciences

- **Diploma in Forensic Science**
- **Diploma in Food Technology**
- **Diploma in Textile Technology**
- **Diploma in Agriculture**
- **Diploma in Horticulture**

- **Diploma in Environmental Science**

4. Diploma in Information Technology and Computer Science

- **Diploma in Computer Science**
- **Diploma in Information Technology**
- **Diploma in Animation and Multimedia**
- **Diploma in Web Development**
- **Diploma in Data Science**

5. Diploma in Laboratory Technology

- **Diploma in Clinical Laboratory Technology**
- **Diploma in Medical Imaging Technology**
- **Diploma in Biochemistry Technology**

6. Diploma in Environmental Management

- A diploma focusing on environmental laws, policies, and sustainable practices.

7. Diploma in Veterinary Sciences

- Focus on animal health, care, and veterinary assistance.

Short-term and Certification Courses

- Certificate in Genomic Sciences
- Certificate in Biotech Lab Technology
- Certificate in Agricultural Science
- Certificate in Environmental Management

- Certificate in Food Safety and Quality Management
- Certificate in Clinical Research
- Certificate in Data Science and Big Data Analytics
- Certificate in Artificial Intelligence

Entrance exams play a crucial role in securing admission to undergraduate (UG) and postgraduate (PG) programs in the science stream. These exams help universities and colleges assess students' knowledge and aptitude in specific scientific subjects. Here's a list of popular entrance exams for UG and PG programs in the science stream:

UG Entrance Exams for Science Stream

1. Joint Entrance Examination (JEE) Main
    - For: Admission to B.Tech/B.E. courses in NITs, IIITs, and other central and state government colleges.
    - Subjects: Physics, Chemistry, Mathematics.
    - Conducted by: National Testing Agency (NTA).
2. JEE Advanced
    - For: Admission to undergraduate courses (B.Tech) at Indian Institutes of Technology (IITs).

- Subjects: Physics, Chemistry, Mathematics.
- Conducted by: IITs.

3. National Eligibility cum Entrance Test (NEET)
   - For: Admission to MBBS, BDS, and other medical courses in government and private medical colleges.
   - Subjects: Physics, Chemistry, Biology.
   - Conducted by: National Testing Agency (NTA).
4. BITSAT (Birla Institute of Technology and Science Admission Test)
   - For: Admission to B.Tech programs at BITS Pilani and its campuses in Goa and Hyderabad.
   - Subjects: Physics, Chemistry, Mathematics, English Proficiency.
   - Conducted by: BITS Pilani.
5. AIIMS Entrance Exam (Undergraduate)
   - For: Admission to MBBS programs at AIIMS institutions.
   - Subjects: Physics, Chemistry, Biology, General Knowledge, Aptitude.
   - Conducted by: All India Institute of Medical Sciences (AIIMS).

6. UPSC Combined Medical Services (CMS) Exam
   - For: Admission to various medical services, especially for candidates pursuing postgraduate programs.
   - Subjects: General Medicine, Pediatrics, Surgery, Obstetrics & Gynecology, etc.
   - Conducted by: Union Public Service Commission (UPSC).
7. KIITEE (Kalinga Institute of Industrial Technology Entrance Examination)
   - For: Admission to B.Tech, B.Sc., and other undergraduate science courses.
   - Subjects: Physics, Chemistry, Mathematics/Biology.
   - Conducted by: KIIT University.
8. NATA (National Aptitude Test in Architecture)
   - For: Admission to undergraduate courses in Architecture.
   - Subjects: Mathematics, General Aptitude, Drawing Test.
   - Conducted by: Council of Architecture.
9. State-Level Entrance Exams
   - For: Admission to UG science courses in state colleges and universities.
   - Examples:

- MHT CET (Maharashtra)
- WBJEE (West Bengal)
- KCET (Karnataka)
- TS EAMCET (Telangana)

  - Subjects: Physics, Chemistry, Mathematics/Biology (depending on the stream).

10. Delhi University Entrance Exam (DUET)
    - For: Admission to various undergraduate science courses (B.Sc.) in Delhi University.
    - Subjects: Varies based on the specific program (e.g., Physics, Chemistry, Biology, Mathematics).
    - Conducted by: University of Delhi.

PG Entrance Exams for Science Stream

1. Graduate Aptitude Test in Engineering (GATE)
    - For: Admission to M.Tech and other postgraduate engineering programs.
    - Subjects: Varies by stream (e.g., Physics, Chemistry, Mathematics, Computer Science).
    - Conducted by: IITs and IISc.

2. National Eligibility Test (NET)
    - For: Eligibility for Junior Research Fellowship (JRF) and Assistant Professor positions, and admission to PG programs in some institutes.
    - Subjects: Physics, Chemistry, Life Sciences, Mathematics, and others.
    - Conducted by: National Testing Agency (NTA).
3. AIIMS PG Entrance Exam
    - For: Admission to MD/MS/PG Diploma programs at AIIMS institutions.
    - Subjects: Medical-related subjects (depending on specialization).
    - Conducted by: All India Institute of Medical Sciences (AIIMS).
4. JAM (Joint Admission Test for M.Sc.)
    - For: Admission to M.Sc. and other post-graduate science programs at IITs and IISc.
    - Subjects: Physics, Chemistry, Mathematics, Biology.
    - Conducted by: IITs.

5. DUET (Delhi University Entrance Test)
    - For: Admission to various PG science courses at Delhi University.
    - Subjects: Varies based on the specific program.
    - Conducted by: University of Delhi.
6. PG Medical Entrance Exam (NEET PG)
    - For: Admission to MD, MS, and PG Diploma programs in medical colleges.
    - Subjects: Medical subjects.
    - Conducted by: National Testing Agency (NTA).
7. BITS Pilani PG Entrance Exam
    - For: Admission to M.Tech, M.Sc. programs at BITS Pilani.
    - Subjects: Depending on the course (e.g., Physics, Chemistry, Mathematics).
    - Conducted by: BITS Pilani.
8. IISc Entrance Exam
    - For: Admission to M.Tech and other postgraduate science and engineering programs.
    - Subjects: Physics, Chemistry, Mathematics.

    - Conducted by: Indian Institute of Science (IISc).
9. State-Level PG Entrance Exams
    - For: Admission to PG science programs in state universities.
    - Examples:
        - MAH CET (Maharashtra)
        - AP PGECET (Andhra Pradesh)
        - TNSET (Tamil Nadu)
    - Subjects: Varies based on the stream and program.
10. CET for Postgraduate Programs
    - For: Admission to postgraduate science courses at various universities (e.g., M.Sc.).
    - Subjects: Subject-specific (Physics, Chemistry, Biology, etc.).

Arts / Humanities:

The Arts or Humanities stream is one of the most versatile and diverse educational paths, offering a broad range of subjects that focus on understanding human society, culture, history, and creative expression. It is an ideal choice for students who are interested in exploring the world through literature, social sciences, philosophy, politics, history, and the arts.

Key Characteristics of the Arts Stream:

- Focus on Creativity and Critical Thinking: The Arts stream encourages creativity, critical analysis, and problem-solving. Students develop skills in communication, writing, research, and argumentation.
- Diverse Subjects: Students can choose from a wide array of subjects, from languages and literature to history, psychology, sociology, philosophy, and more.
- Career Flexibility: The subjects in the Arts stream provide a strong foundation for careers in many fields, such as law, journalism, education, social services, marketing, design, arts, and media.

Here's a list of some well-known career options for students in the Arts and Humanities stream:

1. Journalism and Mass Communication

- Journalist
- News Anchor
- Content Writer
- Digital Marketing Specialist

2. Law

- Corporate Lawyer
- Criminal Lawyer
- Legal Advisor

- Public Prosecutor

3. Education

- Teacher
- Academic Counselor
- Education Consultant
- Research Scholar

4. Design and Creative Arts

- Fashion Designer
- Interior Designer
- Graphic Designer
- Multimedia Artist

5. Psychology and Counseling

- Clinical Psychologist
- Career Counselor
- Child Psychologist
- Organizational Psychologist

6. Performing Arts

- Actor
- Dancer
- Musician
- Theater Artist

7. Social Sciences

- Sociologist
- Historian
- Anthropologist
- Political Scientist

8. Civil Services

- IAS Officer
- IPS Officer
- IFS Officer

9. Writing and Publishing

- Author
- Editor
- Copywriter
- Scriptwriter

10. Languages and Literature

- Translator
- Linguist
- Professor of Literature
- Language Trainer

11. Media and Entertainment

- Film Director
- Producer

- Cinematographer
- Video Editor

12. Event Management

- Event Planner
- Wedding Planner
- Public Relations Specialist

13. Hospitality and Tourism

- Travel Consultant
- Hotel Manager
- Tour Guide

14. Public Administration

- Policy Analyst
- Government Official
- Urban Planner

15. Fine Arts

- Painter
- Sculptor
- Art Curator

Here are some **new-age career options** in the Arts and Humanities stream that are gaining popularity in today's rapidly evolving world:

1. Digital Content Creation

- **YouTuber**
- **Social Media Influencer**
- **Podcaster**
- **Blogger**

2. UX/UI Design

- **User Experience Designer**
- **User Interface Designer**
- **Human-Centered Design Specialist**

3. Creative Technology

- **Virtual Reality (VR) Designer**
- **Augmented Reality (AR) Artist**
- **Interactive Media Specialist**

4. Cultural and Heritage Management

- **Heritage Tourism Expert**
- **Museum Curator**
- **Art Restorer**

5. Sustainability and Social Impact Careers

- **Sustainability Consultant**
- **Social Entrepreneur**
- **NGO Manager**

6. Behavioral Economics and Market Research

- **Consumer Psychologist**
- **Behavioral Economist**
- **Trend Analyst**

7. Gaming and Esports

- **Game Narrative Designer**
- **Esports Manager**
- **Game Streamer**

8. Film and Media Studies

- **Documentary Filmmaker**
- **Media Analyst**
- **Cinematic Critic**

9. Data-Driven Humanities

- **Digital Humanities Researcher**
- **Cultural Data Analyst**
- **Archivist for Digital Assets**

10. Fashion and Lifestyle Careers

- **Sustainable Fashion Designer**
- **Fashion Blogger**
- **Luxury Brand Manager**

11. Experiential Marketing

- **Brand Storyteller**

- **Experiential Event Designer**
- **Immersive Content Creator**

12. Wellness and Mindfulness Careers

- **Mindfulness Coach**
- **Art Therapist**
- **Wellness Retreat Planner**

13. Creative Writing for Digital Media

- **SEO Content Strategist**
- **Copywriter for Digital Campaigns**
- **Scriptwriter for Web Series**

14. Global and Cultural Studies

- **Global Relations Specialist**
- **Cultural Intelligence Coach**
- **Intercultural Communication Consultant**

15. Intellectual Property and Ethics in Media

- **IP Lawyer**
- **Ethical AI Consultant**
- **Digital Rights Advocate**

Focus on Liberal Arts

The liberal arts encompass a broad spectrum of disciplines that emphasize critical thinking, creativity, and interdisciplinary knowledge. They prepare students not only for specific careers but also for adaptability in a rapidly changing world. Here's an overview of liberal arts as a focus area for career counseling:

What are the liberal arts?

The liberal arts traditionally include humanities, social sciences, natural sciences, and mathematics. Examples of subjects within these fields include:

- Humanities: Literature, Philosophy, History, Languages, Arts.
- Social Sciences: Sociology, Psychology, Political Science, Economics.
- Natural Sciences: Biology, Physics, Chemistry.
- Mathematics: Applied and theoretical mathematics.

Benefits of a Liberal Arts Education

1. Well-Rounded Knowledge: Offers exposure to various disciplines, encouraging holistic development.
2. Critical Thinking and Problem-Solving: Fosters analytical skills essential for decision-making.
3. Effective Communication: Enhances written and verbal communication.
4. Adaptability: Prepares students for multiple career paths in diverse fields.
5. Interdisciplinary Learning: Encourages innovative thinking by connecting different domains.

Careers After a Liberal Arts Education

A liberal arts degree can lead to careers in:

- Education: Teaching, academic research.
- Media & Communication: Journalism, publishing, content creation.
- Public Relations & Marketing: Brand strategy, communications specialist.
- Social Services: Counseling, community development.
- Government & Public Policy: Policy analysis, diplomacy, political consulting.
- Creative Arts: Writing, filmmaking, graphic design.
- Corporate Roles: Human resources, training & development, management consulting.

Undergraduate Entrance Exams

India

1. CUET (Common University Entrance Test):
   - For central universities like DU, BHU, JNU, and others.
   - Tests language, general awareness, and domain-specific subjects.
2. Ashoka University Admission Test:
   - For liberal arts and humanities programs at Ashoka University.
   - Includes critical thinking, aptitude, and on-the-spot essay writing.
3. FLAME University Entrance Exam:
   - For admission to FLAME University's interdisciplinary programs.
   - Tests reasoning, aptitude, and writing skills.
4. Christ University Entrance Test (CUET):
   - For arts and humanities courses.
   - Covers English, reasoning, and general knowledge.
5. Symbiosis Entrance Test (SET):

- Required for liberal arts and humanities programs at Symbiosis International.
- Assesses general English, analytical and logical reasoning, and quantitative aptitude.

6. TISS BAT (Tata Institute of Social Sciences - Bachelor's Admission Test):
   - For undergraduate social sciences programs.
   - Tests English, logical reasoning, and general awareness.

Abroad

1. SAT (Scholastic Assessment Test):
   - Widely accepted for liberal arts and humanities programs in the US.
   - Tests evidence-based reading, writing, and mathematics.
2. ACT (American College Testing):
   - An alternative to SAT, including English, reading, math, science reasoning, and an optional writing test.
3. IB Diploma Program:
   - Strong scores in International Baccalaureate (IB) can qualify students for liberal arts colleges abroad.
4. IELTS/TOEFL:

- Required for non-native English speakers applying to universities abroad.
- Tests English language proficiency.

Postgraduate Entrance Exams

India

1. TISS NET (Tata Institute of Social Sciences National Entrance Test):
   - For postgraduate programs in social work, policy, and humanities.
   - Tests general awareness, English, and analytical ability.
2. DUET (Delhi University Entrance Test):
   - For master's programs in humanities disciplines.
   - Tests subject-specific knowledge, reasoning, and language.
3. JNU Entrance Exam (JNUEE):
   - For master's courses in arts and humanities.
   - Focuses on specific subjects like international relations, history, or linguistics.
4. CUET-PG (Common University Entrance Test for PG):
   - For central universities' postgraduate programs.

- Domain-specific tests plus general aptitude.

Abroad

1. GRE (Graduate Record Examination):
   - Required for arts and humanities master's programs in the US and other countries.
   - Tests analytical writing, verbal reasoning, and quantitative reasoning.
2. IELTS/TOEFL:
   - Mandatory for international postgraduate programs for non-native speakers.
3. GMAT (Graduate Management Admission Test):
   - For specific interdisciplinary programs combining management and humanities.
4. Subject-Specific Tests:
   - E.g., GRE Subject Tests for literature in English.

Additional Tips for Students

- Portfolio/Essay Requirements: Some arts and humanities programs require a personal statement, essays, or portfolios.

- Interviews: Universities like Ashoka and FLAME often include an interview round.
- Preparatory Courses: Students can use online platforms like Unacademy, BYJU'S, or Kaplan for preparation.

Creative Arts

1. Diploma in Fine Arts
    - Focus: Painting, sculpture, sketching, and art history.
    - Careers: Artist, illustrator, art director, curator.
2. Diploma in Performing Arts
    - Focus: Music, dance, theater, and acting.
    - Careers: Performer, director, choreographer, event coordinator.
3. Diploma in Graphic Design
    - Focus: Visual communication, design principles, and digital tools.
    - Careers: Graphic designer, UI/UX designer, animator.

Languages and Literature

4. Diploma in English Language and Literature
    - Focus: English literature, creative writing, and communication skills.

- Careers: Writer, editor, teacher, content creator.

5. Diploma in Regional or Foreign Languages
   - Focus: Mastery of languages like French, Spanish, German, or regional languages.
   - Careers: Translator, interpreter, language trainer, international relations professional.

History, Culture, and Society

6. Diploma in History and Archaeology
   - Focus: Historical studies, cultural heritage, and archaeological methods.
   - Careers: Historian, archaeologist, museum curator.
7. Diploma in Sociology and Social Work
   - Focus: Social behavior, community development, and welfare.
   - Careers: Social worker, counselor, NGO worker.
8. Diploma in Philosophy and Ethics
   - Focus: Philosophy, ethical reasoning, and critical thinking.
   - Careers: Academic, ethicist, policy advisor.

Media and Communication

9. Diploma in Journalism and Mass Communication
    - Focus: News writing, reporting, and media studies.
    - Careers: Journalist, news editor, PR specialist.
10. Diploma in Film Studies and Screenwriting
    - Focus: Film history, scriptwriting, and production.
    - Careers: Screenwriter, filmmaker, film critic.

Specialized Areas

11. Diploma in Women's Studies
    - Focus: Gender studies, women's rights, and advocacy.
    - Careers: Gender consultant, social researcher, policy analyst.
12. Diploma in Cultural Studies
    - Focus: Understanding culture through literature, arts, and social sciences.
    - Careers: Cultural analyst, heritage manager, arts program coordinator.

Interdisciplinary Options

13. Diploma in Liberal Arts
    - Focus: Combines multiple disciplines like history, literature, and philosophy.
    - Careers: Generalist roles in education, consulting, or public service.
14. Diploma in Arts Management
    - Focus: Management of arts organizations, events, and cultural projects.
    - Careers: Arts administrator, gallery manager, cultural entrepreneur.

Online and Specialized Programs

15. Diploma in Creative Writing
    - **Offered by platforms like Coursera or university online programs.**
    - **Careers: Writer, editor, content strategist.**
16. Diploma in Ethics and Leadership
    - **Focus: Leadership skills with a philosophical approach.**
    - **Careers: Leadership coach, corporate trainer.**

Key Pathways in Defense

1. Armed Forces
   - Indian Army
     - Roles: Infantry, artillery, engineering corps, medical corps, logistics.
     - Entry Levels:
       - National Defence Academy (NDA): After 12th grade.
       - Combined Defence Services (CDS): After graduation.
       - Technical Entry Scheme (TES): For engineering graduates.
   - Indian Navy
     - Roles: Naval operations, aviation, submarines, logistics, engineering.
     - Entry Levels: NDA, CDS, or Short Service Commission (SSC) for specialized roles.
   - Indian Air Force
     - Roles: Fighter pilots, ground duty officers, technical officers.
     - Entry Levels: NDA, CDS, or Air Force Common Admission Test (AFCAT).

2. Paramilitary Forces

- Forces: Border Security Force (BSF), Central Reserve Police Force (CRPF), Indo-Tibetan Border Police (ITBP), and others.
- Roles: Border protection, internal security, disaster management.
- Entry: Recruitment through Staff Selection Commission (SSC) or UPSC.

3. Defense Research and Development

- Defense Research and Development Organisation (DRDO):
    - Roles: Scientists, engineers, and technical staff working on advanced defense technologies.
    - Eligibility: Engineering or science degrees; entry through DRDO's Scientist Entry Test (SET).

4. Defense Engineering

- Roles: Designing and maintaining defense equipment like ships, aircraft, and weapon systems.
- Pathways: Entry through defense contractors like Hindustan Aeronautics Limited (HAL) or Bharat Electronics Limited (BEL).

5. Administrative and Intelligence Roles

- Roles: Intelligence analysts (RAW, IB), defense administrative officers.
- Entry: Civil services exams or specialized recruitment.

How to Prepare for a Career in Defense

Education:

- For officer roles: A 10+2, graduation, or engineering degree is required.
- For technical roles: Focus on STEM fields.

Physical Fitness:

- Develop endurance, strength, and overall fitness. Physical exams are mandatory.

Competitive Exams:

- NDA Exam (10+2 level)
- CDS Exam (for graduates)
- AFCAT (for Air Force roles)
- Technical entry schemes for engineers.

Personality Development:

- Leadership, teamwork, and quick decision-making are crucial.
- Train for the Service Selection Board (SSB) interviews.

Skills Needed

1. Discipline and resilience.
2. Teamwork and adaptability.
3. Analytical thinking and problem-solving.
4. Technical knowledge for specialized roles.

Perks of a Career in Defense

1. Job Security: Permanent commission or short service commission options.
2. Pay and Benefits: Competitive salary, allowances, pensions, medical benefits, housing, and education for children.
3. Adventure and Respect: Opportunities to serve on challenging missions and earn national recognition.

Key Institutes

- National Defence Academy (NDA), Pune
- Indian Military Academy (IMA), Dehradun
- Air Force Academy, Dundigal
- Naval Academy, Ezhimala
- Officers Training Academy (OTA), Chennai and Gaya

Career In Security / Asset Management / Fire safety

A career in private security, loss prevention, fire safety, and personal security offers exciting opportunities in safeguarding assets, preventing risks, and ensuring the safety of people and properties. Certifications like Certified Protection Professional (CPP) and NEBOSH (National Examination Board in Occupational Safety and Health) add credibility and expertise to professionals in this field.

Career Pathways

1. Private Security Management
   - Roles:
     - Security Consultant
     - Security Operations Manager
     - Risk Analyst
     - Security Trainer
   - Responsibilities:
     - Developing security plans for organizations.
     - Managing security personnel and operations.
     - Conducting risk assessments and audits.
2. Loss Prevention
   - Roles:
     - Loss Prevention Officer/Manager
     - Retail Security Specialist

- Responsibilities:
    - Protecting assets and reducing shrinkage in retail or logistics.
    - Investigating theft, fraud, and policy violations.
    - Implementing surveillance systems and policies.

3. Fire Safety and Risk Management

- Roles:
    - Fire Safety Officer/Manager
    - Health and Safety Consultant
- Responsibilities:
    - Conducting fire risk assessments and audits.
    - Ensuring compliance with fire safety regulations.
    - Training employees in emergency preparedness.

4. Personal Security (Close Protection)

- Roles:
    - Personal Security Officer (PSO)
    - Executive Protection Specialist

- Responsibilities:
    - Protecting high-profile clients (e.g., executives, celebrities).
    - Conducting threat assessments and planning safe movements.
    - Providing physical protection and situational awareness.

5. Corporate Security

- Roles:
    - Corporate Security Manager
    - Crisis Management Specialist
- Responsibilities:
    - Managing internal security for corporations.
    - Overseeing crisis response and continuity planning.
    - Implementing policies for employee and data security.

Certifications to Boost Your Career

1. Certified Protection Professional (CPP)

- Offered by ASIS International.
- Focus: Security management, investigations, threat analysis.
- Eligibility: Experience in security management (typically 7+ years).

- Benefits:
    - Recognized globally.
    - Opens senior roles like Security Director or Consultant.

2. NEBOSH Certifications

- Focus: Occupational health, safety, and environmental management.
- Popular Courses:
    - NEBOSH General Certificate: Entry-level for health and safety professionals.
    - NEBOSH Fire Certificate: Specialized in fire risk management.
- Benefits:
    - Compliance with international safety standards.
    - Opportunities in risk assessment and HSE (Health, Safety, and Environment) roles.

3. Other Relevant Certifications

- Certified Fire Protection Specialist (CFPS): Specializes in fire safety.
- Close Protection Training: Offered by certified security agencies for personal security roles.
- Certified Security Consultant (CSC): For consultants providing security solutions.

- First Aid and CPR Certification: Essential for fire and safety roles.

Skills Needed

1. Technical Knowledge: Understanding of security systems, fire prevention methods, and risk management.
2. Analytical Thinking: Identifying vulnerabilities and mitigating risks.
3. Leadership: Managing security teams and training personnel.
4. Communication: Handling clients and reporting incidents clearly.
5. Physical Fitness: Important for roles in personal security and fire safety.

Industries and Employers

- Industries:
    - Corporate security and business parks.
    - Retail chains and logistics companies.
    - Hospitality and events.
    - Private security firms.
    - Critical infrastructure (oil & gas, power plants).
- Major Employers:
    - G4S, Securitas, and Allied Universal (global security firms).

    - Corporate giants like Google, Amazon, and financial institutions.
    - Government contractors for sensitive facilities.

Salary Expectations

- Entry Level: $25,000–$40,000 per year.
- Mid-Level (with CPP/NEBOSH): $50,000–$90,000 per year.
- Senior-Level (Security Director/Consultant): $100,000+ per year.

How to Get Started

1. Education: Diploma or degree in security management, fire safety, or related fields.
2. Certifications: Pursue CPP, NEBOSH, or specialized courses.
3. Experience: Work with security firms or in-house security departments.
4. Networking: Join professional organizations like ASIS International.

Would you like tailored advice on certifications, job opportunities, or further studies in this field?

Study Abroad Guide: How to Apply Abroad

Studying abroad can be an enriching experience, opening doors to global education, cultural exposure, and career opportunities. Here's a step-by-step guide to applying to universities or colleges abroad:

1. Research and Choose Your Destination

- Top Destinations: USA, UK, Canada, Australia, Germany, France, etc.
- Factors to Consider:
  - Language of instruction.
  - Tuition fees and living costs.
  - Post-study work opportunities.
  - Course options and university rankings.

2. Select a Program

- Research programs based on your interests and career goals.
- Check prerequisites like specific academic qualifications, entrance exams, or work experience (if applicable).

- Use platforms like QS Rankings, Times Higher Education, or university websites to compare courses.

3. Meet Admission Requirements

- Academic Transcripts: Submit transcripts from previous schools/colleges.
- Standardized Tests (if required):
    - Undergraduate Programs: SAT, ACT.
    - Postgraduate Programs: GRE, GMAT.
- English Language Proficiency Tests:
    - TOEFL, IELTS, or PTE (depending on country/university).

4. Prepare Application Documents

- Statement of Purpose (SOP): Explains why you want to join the program and your career goals.
- Letters of Recommendation (LOR): From teachers, employers, or mentors.
- CV/Resume: Highlights academic, extracurricular, and work achievements.
- Portfolio: For creative courses (e.g., design, architecture).

5. Apply to Universities

- Most universities accept applications online.
- Apply directly through the university's website or centralized platforms like:

- UCAS (UK)
- Common App (USA)
- DAAD (Germany)
- Studielink (Netherlands).

- Check deadlines carefully. Some universities have early and regular decision timelines.

6. Take Care of Financial Planning

- Tuition Fees: Research costs and available scholarships.
- Financial Aid and Scholarships:
    - Apply for need-based or merit-based scholarships.
    - Explore government-funded opportunities like Chevening (UK), DAAD (Germany), or Fulbright (USA).
- Student Loans: Check for education loans from banks or financial institutions.

7. Apply for a Student Visa

- After receiving an admission offer, apply for a student visa.
- Requirements:
    - Proof of acceptance from the university.
    - Financial documents showing ability to cover expenses.
    - Valid passport and health insurance.

- Visa Types:
    - F-1 Visa (USA).
    - Tier 4 Student Visa (UK).
    - Subclass 500 (Australia).

8. Arrange Accommodation and Travel

- Accommodation Options: On-campus housing, private rentals, or shared apartments.
- Travel Planning:
    - Book flights early to save costs.
    - Check for student discounts and baggage allowances.

9. Prepare for Departure

- Pre-Departure Checklist:
    - Health check-ups and vaccinations (if required).
    - Open an international student bank account.
    - Familiarize yourself with local culture and laws.
- Attend orientation programs offered by the university.

10. Post-Arrival Steps

- Register with local authorities (if required).

- Get your student ID and set up utilities (if living off-campus).
- Join student groups and participate in activities to adapt to the new environment.

Additional Tips

1. Start Early: Begin planning at least 12-18 months before the intended start date.
2. Consult Experts: Reach out to education consultants for guidance on applications and visas.
3. Use Online Resources: Websites like Studyportals, IDP, or university guides help with detailed program and country information.

What is an Early Application?

An Early Application is a process that allows students to apply to universities or colleges before the regular application deadlines. Early applications typically have deadlines between October and November of the year before the intended start date of college. They are commonly used by students who are clear about their top-choice universities.

Types of Early Applications

1. Early Decision (ED):
    - Binding: If accepted, you must attend the institution and withdraw applications to other universities.

- Suitable for students who are 100% sure about their first-choice college.
- Example: Ivy League schools in the USA often offer ED.

2. Early Action (EA):
    - Non-binding: You can apply to other universities and are not obligated to attend if accepted.
    - Allows students to receive decisions early but still decide by the regular decision deadline.
    - Example: Many US universities, like the University of Chicago and MIT, offer EA.
3. Restrictive/Single-Choice Early Action (REA):
    - Non-binding: Similar to Early Action but limits the number of other schools to which you can apply early.
    - Example: Stanford University and Harvard University offer REA.

Advantages of Early Applications

1. Early Decision Notification:
    - Early applicants typically receive decisions by December, giving peace of mind or time to adjust plans.

2. Higher Acceptance Rates:
    - Some universities have slightly higher acceptance rates for early applicants, as they prioritize students committed to their institution.
3. Demonstrates Commitment:
    - Applying early shows the university that you are genuinely interested in their program.
4. More Time for Preparation:
    - Early admission allows you to focus on financial aid, scholarships, and other preparations if accepted.

Considerations Before Applying Early

1. Strong Academic Profile:
    - Your grades and standardized test scores (if applicable) must be competitive by the early application deadline.
2. Preparedness:
    - Ensure your application, including the Statement of Purpose (SOP), Letters of Recommendation (LOR), and other documents, is ready by October or November.

3. Commitment (for ED):
    - Be 100% sure about the university if applying through Early Decision since it is binding.
4. Limitations:
    - For EA and REA, you may need to wait for regular decision timelines for other schools to finalize your choice.

Timeline for Early Applications

1. 12-18 Months Before Deadline:
    - Research universities and programs.
    - Begin preparing for standardized tests (SAT, ACT, TOEFL, etc.).
2. 10-12 Months Before Deadline:
    - Shortlist universities and understand their early application policies.
    - Draft SOPs and request LORs from teachers or mentors.
3. 6-9 Months Before Deadline:
    - Complete and finalize your application.
    - Apply by the early application deadline (usually October/November).
4. 1-2 Months After Submission:
    - Receive decisions (typically by December).

How to Write a Statement of Purpose (SOP)

A Statement of Purpose (SOP) is an essential part of your application to universities or colleges, particularly for postgraduate programs. It serves as an introduction to your goals, academic background, and motivations. Here's a structured approach to writing an effective SOP:

1. Understand the Purpose of an SOP

- The SOP is a chance for you to explain why you are applying, what you intend to study, and how it aligns with your career goals.
- It gives the admissions committee insight into your personality, goals, and potential to contribute to the university community.

2. SOP Structure

1. Introduction (1-2 Paragraphs)
    - Start with a Hook: A personal anecdote, experience, or moment that inspired your interest in the field.
    - Example: "Ever since I was a child, I have been fascinated by how technology can solve real-world problems, especially in healthcare."
    - State Your Purpose: Clearly mention what program you are applying for and why.

- Example: "This passion led me to pursue a degree in Biomedical Engineering, and now, I am eager to further my studies at [University Name] to gain the skills necessary to contribute to cutting-edge healthcare innovations."

2. Academic Background (2-3 Paragraphs)
   - Discuss Your Previous Education: Highlight relevant academic achievements, courses, and projects that prepared you for the program.
   - Skills and Knowledge: Show how your academic background aligns with the program and how it lays the foundation for future success.
   - Example: "During my undergraduate years, I worked on a project where I used AI algorithms to predict patient outcomes, which deepened my interest in applying machine learning in medical fields."
3. Professional Experience (1-2 Paragraphs)
   - Work/Internships: Mention any relevant internships, work experience, or research projects.
   - Skills and Accomplishments: Highlight key achievements, challenges, and how

they contributed to your professional growth.

  - Example: "During my internship at XYZ Company, I developed a prototype for a wearable health monitoring device, gaining valuable hands-on experience in product development."

4. Why This Program and University (2-3 Paragraphs)
   - Why the Program: Discuss what draws you to the program, including specific courses, professors, or research opportunities.
   - Why This University: Mention why this university is a good fit for your academic and career goals (location, resources, reputation).
   - Example: "The unique opportunity to work with Dr. [Name], whose research on AI in healthcare aligns with my aspirations, is a major reason why I am applying to [University Name]."
5. Future Goals (1-2 Paragraphs)
   - Career Aspirations: Explain how this program will help you achieve your long-term career goals.
   - Contribution to the Field: Show how you plan to contribute to the field or

make an impact with the knowledge you gain.

  - Example: "After completing the program, I aim to work in a technology-driven healthcare company, applying AI to improve patient outcomes, and ultimately make healthcare more accessible."

6. Conclusion (1 Paragraph)
   - Reaffirm Your Commitment: Summarize your goals and express your enthusiasm for joining the program.
   - Example: "I am confident that the [University Name] program will provide me with the skills, knowledge, and experience needed to achieve my career goals and contribute to the field of biomedical engineering."

3. Tips for Writing a Strong SOP

- Be Clear and Concise: Stick to the word limit (usually 1000-1500 words).
- Show, Don't Tell: Use examples from your life or experiences to demonstrate your skills and passion.
- Customize Your SOP: Tailor it for each university and program.

- Be Honest: Avoid exaggerating or fabricating experiences. Authenticity resonates.
- Proofread: Review for grammar, punctuation, and coherence.

How to Write a Personal Story for Your SOP

A personal story is an essential part of your SOP, as it helps create a connection with the admissions committee. It should illustrate your passion for the field, your background, and the experiences that shaped your decision to pursue this program.

1. Identify the Core Message

- Think about an experience that motivated your interest in the field you want to study.
- This could be a specific moment, challenge, or realization during your education, work, or personal life.
- Example: "The moment I realized the potential of artificial intelligence in improving healthcare came when I witnessed a friend's father struggle with the inefficiencies of medical diagnosis."

2. Be Authentic

- Share a true and meaningful story from your life. The more personal and reflective it is, the better it will resonate.

- Avoid Clichés: Try not to rely on overused examples unless they truly reflect your unique experience.

3. Connect the Story to Your Goals

- Relate the personal story to your academic journey and career aspirations.
- Example: "That experience sparked my curiosity in AI, leading me to pursue a degree in computer science, and now, I am eager to apply this knowledge to the healthcare industry."

4. Keep it Relevant

- The personal story should tie directly to your goals and the program you're applying for.
- Avoid irrelevant details or long narratives that distract from your purpose.

5. Reflect and End on a Positive Note

- Reflect on what you learned from the experience and how it shaped you.
- End the story with a forward-looking statement about your aspirations and how the program will help you achieve them.
- Example: "This journey has taught me the importance of combining technology with empathy, and I am excited to develop my skills further at [University Name] to make a meaningful impact in healthcare."

Tips for Crafting a Personal Story

- Be Vulnerable: Share a challenge or setback, but focus on how it led to growth or insight.
- Be Relatable: Admissions officers are human. If they can relate to your story, it's more impactful.
- Keep it Balanced: Include both personal elements and academic achievements to show how they complement each other.

Would you like help brainstorming a personal story or feedback on an existing SOP draft?

Here are some important templates that can help students stay organized, track their progress, and enhance their study habits. These templates are useful for planning, goal setting, and time management, among other areas.

1. Study Schedule Template

A study schedule helps students allocate time for different subjects or tasks. This template is perfect for managing time effectively.

Day/Time	Subject/Activity	Duration	Notes
Monday	Math (Chapter 1)	1 hour	Review examples
	History (Timeline review)	1 hour	Focus on key events
Tuesday	English (Reading & Writing)	1.5 hours	Practice essay writing
Wednesday	Chemistry (Experiment prep)	1 hour	Memorize formulas
Thursday	Physics (Unit Test Revision)	1 hour	Practice questions
Friday	Revision (All subjects)	2 hours	Revise weak areas

2. Daily Study Plan Template

A daily study plan breaks down tasks into smaller chunks and allows students to prioritize them effectively.

Time	Task	Priority	Completed
7:00 AM	Wake up and breakfast	Low	
8:00 AM	Revise Math formulas	High	

9:00 AM	History reading	Medium	
10:30 AM	Break	Low	
11:00 AM	Chemistry experiment notes review	High	
12:00 PM	Lunch break	Low	
1:00 PM	Write English essay	High	
3:00 PM	Review Physics chapter on waves	Medium	
4:00 PM	Break	Low	
4:30 PM	Practice test for upcoming exam	High	
6:00 PM	Relax and review day's progress	Low	

3. Weekly Study Plan Template

A weekly study plan helps students organize their entire week in advance, balancing study with other activities.

Day	Subject/ Activity	Goals for the Day	Completed
Monday	Math (Chapter 1)	Complete 5 practice problems	
	History (World Wars)	Study key events and causes	
Tuesday	English (Writing Essay)	Write first draft of essay	
	Chemistry (Reactions)	Read and note down reactions	
Wednesday	Physics (Mechanics)	Understand Newton's laws	
	Geography (Landforms)	Draw and label maps	
Thursday	Math (Algebra)	Complete homework assignments	
	Biology (Cell structure)	Create a diagram	
Friday	English (Poetry)	Study 2 poems and	

		write analysis	
	History (Revolutionary movements)	Create flashcards for key figures	

4. Goal Setting Template

Goal setting helps students stay focused on their long-term and short-term objectives. This template can guide students in setting and tracking their goals.

Goal	Specific Actions	Deadline	Progress
Improve Math Skills	Complete 3 chapters, solve 20 practice problems	2 weeks from now	10% completed
Finish English Essay	Research topics, write draft, revise draft	1 week from now	50% completed
Pass Upcoming Physics Exam	Revise Chapters 3–5, complete practice tests	2 weeks from now	20% completed
Learn French Vocabulary	Study 10 new words daily	Ongoing	30% completed

5. Revision Checklist Template

A revision checklist helps students ensure they cover all topics before exams or assessments.

Subject	Topic	Completed	Comments/Notes
Math	Chapter 1: Algebra	✔	Understand concepts
	Chapter 2: Geometry	✕	Review formulas
English	Grammar	✔	Practice exercises
	Essay writing	✔	Draft essay
Physics	Newton's Laws	✔	Solve example problems
	Energy and Work	✕	Focus on theory
Chemistry	Atomic Structure	✔	Review key concepts
	Periodic Table	✔	Memorize elements

6. Study Progress Tracker Template

A progress tracker helps students keep track of what they've completed and what's pending.

Date	Subject/Activity	Time Spent	Completion Status	Notes
Dec 1	Math (Chapter 1: Algebra)	2 hours	100% completed	Mastered concepts
Dec 2	History (World War I)	1.5 hours	80% completed	Need to finish reading
Dec 3	Chemistry (Periodic Table)	1 hour	90% completed	Need more practice
Dec 4	English (Essay Writing)	2 hours	50% completed	Draft completed

7. Motivation Tracker Template

Tracking motivation and focus can help students stay on track when their energy wanes.

Week/ Date	Motivation Level	Key Achievements	Challenges
Week 1	8/10	Completed all assignments	Felt overwhelmed with workload
Week 2	7/10	Finished major revision	Struggled with keeping focus

Week 3	9/10	Improved grades in Math	Had difficulty managing time

8. Time Blocking Template

Time blocking helps students allocate specific time slots for different study tasks or subjects.

Time Block	Activity	Duration	Priority
7:00 AM - 9:00 AM	Math Practice	2 hours	High
9:00 AM - 10:00 AM	Break/Rest	1 hour	Low
10:00 AM - 12:00 PM	History Revision	2 hours	Medium
12:00 PM - 1:00 PM	Lunch	1 hour	Low
1:00 PM - 3:00 PM	English Essay Writing	2 hours	High
3:00 PM - 5:00 PM	Chemistry Study	2 hours	Medium

These templates can help streamline a student's study routine, keep track of progress, and improve overall productivity. Would you like to customize any of these templates further or need assistance with a specific one?

Here are the templates you requested for organizing goals, career mapping, profile building, SWOT analysis, and performance tracking.

Template 1: My Goals

This template helps you clearly define and track your personal and professional goals.

Goal	Specific Actions/ Steps	Deadline	Priority	Progress	Notes
Personal Goal: Improve time management	1. Create a daily schedule 2. Stick to time blocks 3. Reflect weekly	3 months from now	High	In Progress	Need to improve in the evenings
Career Goal: Gain a promotion	1. Learn new skills 2. Take on leadership projects 3. Seek feedback	6 months from now	High	Not Started	Plan to start a leadership course
Educational Goal: Complete a certification	1. Research courses 2. Register and complete assignments	2 months from now	Medium	20% Completed	Need to finalize course selection

Template 2: My Career Map

A career map helps you outline the steps to achieve your career aspirations, along with short-term and long-term goals.

Stage	Goal/ Objective	Skills/ Experiences Needed	Action Steps	Timeline	Progress
Current Position	Security Specialist Consultant	Security management expertise	Finalize projects, gain more corporate clients	6 months	Ongoing
Short-Term Goal	Become a Center Manager in a wellness startup	Leadership, clinic operations	Apply for positions, network with industry experts	1 year	In Progress
Long-Term Goal	Lead a security operations department in a large corporation	Strategic planning, team leadership	Prepare for higher education, take on strategic roles	3-5 years	Not Started

Template 3: Profile Building Map

A profile building map outlines the steps to enhance your personal or professional brand, which is critical for career progression.

Area	Action Steps	Target Deadline	Resources/ Support Needed	Progress
Skills Development	1. Enroll in leadership training 2. Take a public speaking course	6 months	Online courses, mentors	In Progress
Networking	1. Attend industry conferences 2. Join profession al groups	3-6 months	Event platforms, LinkedIn	Ongoing
Online Presence	1. Update LinkedIn profile 2. Start a profession al blog	1 month	LinkedIn, personal website	50% completed
Certifications	1. Gain certification in project management	6 months	Certification courses	Not Started

Template 4: My SWOT Analysis

A SWOT analysis helps you assess your Strengths, Weaknesses, Opportunities, and Threats in both personal and professional life.

Category	Details
Strengths	1. Strong analytical skills 2. Ability to work under pressure 3. Effective communicator
Weaknesses	1. Limited experience in leadership roles 2. Need to improve delegation skills
Opportunities	1. Upcoming industry trend in AI-driven security 2. Leadership training programs
Threats	1. Increased competition in the security industry 2. Changes in technology could require upskilling

Template 5: My Performance Tracker

A performance tracker helps you monitor your progress toward goals and objectives, making it easier to identify areas for improvement.

Date	Task/ Goal	Time Spent	Outcome/ Result	Challenges/ Notes	Next Steps
Dec 1, 2024	Complete Leadership training module	2 hours	Completed	Some difficulty in understanding concepts	Review additional resources
Dec 5, 2024	Finalize client proposal for security services	3 hours	Proposal sent	Delayed due to client request	Follow up with client
Dec 10, 2024	Write LinkedIn profile summary	1 hour	Completed	Struggled with self-promotion	Seek feedback from mentor

These templates can help you stay organized and on track with your goals, career progression, profile building, and personal growth. Would you like assistance in customizing any of these further or need advice on any of these areas?

Role and Support of Student Needs from Parents & Teachers

Parents and teachers both play critical roles in supporting students' educational and personal development. Their involvement is key to helping students succeed academically, emotionally, and socially. Here's a guide to understanding their roles and how they can support students.

1. Role of Parents in Supporting Students

Emotional Support:

- Encouragement and Motivation: Parents can provide positive reinforcement, encourage a growth mindset, and be a source of comfort during challenging times.
- Listening: Creating an open environment where students feel safe to express their concerns, frustrations, and successes.
- Building Self-Esteem: Recognizing achievements, no matter how small, helps build confidence.

Academic Support:

- Setting Expectations: Encouraging students to set academic goals, and maintain a healthy attitude toward success and failure.

- Time Management: Helping students establish good study habits and organizing their schedules effectively.
- Providing Resources: Supplying necessary tools such as books, technology, or tutors, if needed.

Setting a Positive Example:

- Modeling Lifelong Learning: Parents who are lifelong learners often inspire the same attitude in their children.
- Work-Life Balance: Demonstrating how to balance work and personal time can teach students the importance of self-care.

Communication with Teachers:

- Advocating for the Student: Parents should maintain regular communication with teachers, attending parent-teacher conferences, and ensuring that the student's needs are being met.
- Problem Solving: If a student is facing academic or behavioral challenges, parents can work with teachers to create a plan for improvement.

2. Role of Teachers in Supporting Students

Academic Support:

- Individualized Attention: Teachers can identify each student's strengths and weaknesses and provide tailored resources or extra help.

- Encouraging Critical Thinking: Teachers should foster an environment where students are encouraged to think independently, ask questions, and explore new ideas.
- Providing Constructive Feedback: Regular, actionable feedback helps students improve their performance.

Social and Emotional Support:

- Creating a Safe Environment: Teachers should create a classroom atmosphere where students feel comfortable making mistakes and learning from them.
- Conflict Resolution: Teachers play a role in helping students navigate conflicts with peers or schoolwork and fostering teamwork and collaboration.
- Recognizing Struggles: Teachers can identify emotional or mental health struggles in students and collaborate with counselors or parents to provide support.

Building Strong Relationships:

- Mentorship: Teachers often act as mentors, guiding students not only in their studies but in their personal development.
- Creating a Sense of Belonging: Teachers help students feel valued in the classroom, which increases motivation and engagement.

Collaboration with Parents:

- Regular Communication: Keeping parents informed about their child's progress, challenges, and achievements helps parents support their student's growth.
- Involving Parents in Learning: Teachers can suggest resources, activities, or even share strategies that can be applied at home.

How Parents and Teachers Can Collaborate:

- Regular Updates: Setting up regular communication, whether through parent-teacher meetings, phone calls, or digital platforms.
- Work Together on Solutions: If a student is struggling academically or emotionally, collaboration between parents and teachers can provide a more holistic solution.
- Promote Consistency: Consistent expectations from both home and school create a stable environment for the student.

Guide for Creating Your Own Resume at School

Creating a strong resume during school is an important step toward preparing for internships, part-time jobs, or even applying to colleges. Here's a guide on how students can create their own resume.

1. Start with Your Contact Information

- Full Name: Use your full name as it appears on official documents.
- Phone Number: Use a personal or parental phone number where you can be easily reached.
- Email Address: Create a professional email address if you don't have one (avoid nicknames or inappropriate words).
- LinkedIn Profile or Portfolio (Optional): If you have one, include the link to your LinkedIn profile or an online portfolio showcasing your skills.

2. Write a Strong Objective or Summary (Optional)

This is a brief 2-3 sentence statement that explains what you aim to achieve with your resume. It should focus on your career goals or internship objectives.

Example Objective:

"Motivated high school student seeking a summer internship in digital marketing to apply my passion for social media, graphic design, and content creation."

3. Highlight Your Education

- School Name: Include the full name of your school and the city you're located in.
- Expected Graduation Date: Include the year you expect to graduate.
- Relevant Coursework (Optional): List any courses relevant to the job or internship you're applying for.
- Academic Achievements: Mention GPA if it's strong or any honors and awards you've earned.

Example Education Section:

- High School Name, City, State
- Expected Graduation: May 2025
- GPA: 3.8/4.0
- Relevant Coursework: Introduction to Business, Advanced Math, AP Chemistry

4. Include Relevant Experience

- Internships: Include any internships or volunteer work. Focus on skills and accomplishments.
- Part-time Jobs: Include any paid or unpaid work experience.

- Extracurricular Activities: Involvement in clubs, sports, student government, or any leadership roles.
- Freelance or Personal Projects: If applicable, include freelance work or projects you've completed outside of school.

Example Experience Section:

- Social Media Intern
- *XYZ Company*, City, State | June 2023 - August 2023
    - Managed social media posts and engagement for a growing online business.
    - Assisted in creating promotional materials using graphic design tools like Canva and Photoshop.
- Student Government Treasurer
- *High School*, City, State | September 2022 - Present
    - Managed a budget of $1,000 for school events and activities.
    - Coordinated fundraising campaigns and maintained financial records.

5. Add Skills

- Technical Skills: List any computer skills or software you are proficient in (e.g., Microsoft Office, Google Suite, Adobe Photoshop).
- Language Skills: If you speak more than one language, list them with your proficiency level.
- Soft Skills: Highlight transferable skills like communication, teamwork, leadership, problem-solving, etc.

Example Skills Section:

- Proficient in Microsoft Word, Excel, and PowerPoint
- Fluent in Spanish and English
- Strong communication and team collaboration skills

6. Add Certifications or Awards (Optional)

- If you've earned any certifications or awards, include them here. For example, certifications in First Aid, digital marketing courses, or any academic awards.
- Example:
    - Certified in Google Analytics (2024)
    - Perfect Attendance Award (2023-2024)

7. Keep It Simple and Well-Formatted

- Length: Keep the resume to one page, especially if you're just starting out.
- Fonts: Use easy-to-read fonts like Arial, Calibri, or Times New Roman.
- Bullet Points: Use bullet points for readability, and start each point with an action verb (e.g., organized, led, managed).
- Proofread: Always check for spelling, grammar, and formatting errors before submitting.

This resume guide can help students structure their resumes to highlight their strengths, experience, and skills effectively. Would you like assistance in refining your resume or need help with another part of the process?

Frequently Asked Questions by Parents

Here are some common questions parents often ask about their child's education, career guidance, and future planning:

1. How can I help my child choose the right career path?

- **Answer**: Encourage your child to explore their interests and strengths through various activities, volunteer work, internships, or part-time jobs. Help them research different career options and consider their skills, passions, and long-term goals. It's also helpful to involve a career counselor who can provide assessments and advice based on their interests and skills.

2. What is the best way to support my child during exam periods?

- **Answer**: Ensure your child has a quiet and comfortable study environment, offer encouragement, and help them create a study schedule that balances work and rest. Encourage good nutrition, exercise, and sleep, as these all contribute to focus and mental health. Show empathy and be patient during high-stress moments.

3. How do I know if my child needs extra academic help?

- **Answer**: If your child is struggling with grades, shows a lack of motivation, or frequently expresses frustration or anxiety about schoolwork, it might indicate that they need extra help. Involve teachers to discuss their progress and determine if tutoring, special learning support, or counseling would be beneficial.

4. How can I manage my child's college application process?

- **Answer**: Start early by helping your child organize and prioritize their application tasks. Ensure they meet deadlines for applications, tests (like SAT, ACT), scholarships, and letters of recommendation. Be supportive and not overbearing, allowing them to take ownership of the process while offering guidance when needed.

5. Should I be concerned if my child is unsure about their career choice?

- **Answer**: It is normal for students to be uncertain about their career path, especially in high school. Support them in exploring different interests and opportunities, such as internships, volunteering, and job shadowing. Encourage open discussions, and remind them that career paths can evolve over time.

6. How do I deal with my child's stress or anxiety related to school or future plans?

- **Answer**: Acknowledge your child's feelings and provide a safe space for them to talk. Help them develop healthy coping strategies like time management, relaxation techniques, and physical activities. If necessary, seek professional help from a counselor or therapist to manage stress or anxiety.

7. What are the best ways to stay involved in my child's school life?

- **Answer**: Attend parent-teacher conferences, volunteer for school events, and maintain regular communication with teachers. Show interest in their homework and projects, and support their extracurricular activities. Be involved but give them the independence they need to grow.

Frequently Asked Questions by Students

Here are some common questions students often ask about their studies, career options, and personal development:

1. How do I choose the right career?

- **Answer**: Start by reflecting on your interests, strengths, and values. Think about what you enjoy doing in your free time, your favorite subjects, and what excites you. Research different career options, seek advice from professionals, and consider taking career assessments. Remember, your career path may evolve, so keep an open mind.

2. What should I include in my resume for my first job or internship?

- **Answer**: Focus on your skills, education, volunteer work, and any extracurricular activities that showcase your strengths. Even if you don't have job experience, emphasize skills like communication, teamwork, leadership, or problem-solving. Make sure your resume is neat, clear, and free of errors.

3. How can I manage my time effectively during school?

- **Answer**: Create a study schedule that includes time for schoolwork, activities, and rest. Break tasks into smaller, manageable chunks, and prioritize your assignments. Use tools like planners or digital apps to stay organized, and make sure to set aside time for self-care.

4. What should I do if I'm struggling with a subject?

- **Answer**: Don't hesitate to ask for help from your teacher, classmates, or a tutor. Study groups can also be beneficial. Break down the material into smaller parts and review consistently. Additionally, consider using online resources or videos that explain the subject in different ways.

5. How can I get more involved in extracurricular activities?

- **Answer**: Research clubs, sports, or volunteer opportunities at your school or in your community. Find something that interests you or challenges you. Extracurricular activities not only enrich your experience but can also build valuable skills that will be useful in your future career.

6. How do I prepare for college or university applications?

- **Answer**: Start by researching potential schools and their application requirements. Keep track of deadlines and necessary documents (such as transcripts, letters of recommendation, and standardized test scores). Focus on making your personal statement or essays authentic and reflective of your experiences and goals. Make sure to prepare for interviews if required.

7. Should I pursue a career I'm passionate about or one that pays well?

- **Answer**: Ideally, you should aim to find a career that aligns with both your passion and your financial needs. It's important to do what you love, but also consider factors like job stability, salary, and long-term growth. If you're uncertain, consider careers that offer both creativity and financial rewards, such as technology, design, or healthcare.

8. How do I stay motivated during tough times in school?

- **Answer**: Remind yourself of your long-term goals and why you're working hard. Break down big tasks into smaller, more manageable steps. Celebrate small victories along the way and keep a support network of friends, family, or teachers who encourage you. Also, find ways to balance work with things you enjoy.

9. What do I do if I don't know what I want to study or do after high school?

- **Answer**: Don't panic—it's okay to be unsure. Take the time to explore different subjects, try internships, and talk to professionals in fields that interest you. You can also pursue general education courses in college or take a gap year to gain more clarity about your future direction.

These FAQs help both parents and students navigate common concerns and challenges in education, career planning, and personal development. Would you like more guidance on any specific question or area?

Letter to Parents:

Subject: Supporting Your Child's Success and Well-Being: A Guide for Parents

Dear Parents,

As your child navigates their educational journey, it is crucial that we work together to ensure their success, both academically and personally. Your involvement and support play an essential role in shaping their future, and by maintaining a strong partnership with their school, we can provide a nurturing environment for their growth.

Supporting Your Child's Career Path Helping your child choose the right career is a collaborative process. Encourage them to explore their interests, strengths, and passions through extracurricular activities, volunteer work, internships, and part-time jobs. The earlier they begin reflecting on their career aspirations, the more clarity they will have as they move forward. If they are uncertain, remind them that career paths can evolve, and it's okay to take time exploring different opportunities.

Providing Emotional and Academic Support During stressful times like exam periods, your support can make a big difference. Acknowledge their feelings and create a conducive environment for studying. Help them organize their time, balance their commitments, and practice self-care. Remember that mental health and emotional well-being are just as important as academic success.

Effective Communication with Teachers Regular communication with your child's teachers is key. Stay updated on their academic progress and any concerns that may arise. By working together, we can identify areas where your child may need extra help, whether it's academic support, time management skills, or social-emotional guidance.

Navigating the College Application Process The college application process can be overwhelming, but it's important to stay organized and informed. Help your child meet deadlines for applications, standardized tests, and required documents. Offer support, but allow them to take ownership of the process, as it's a crucial step in developing independence and responsibility.

Please feel free to reach out if you have any questions or concerns. Let's continue to work together to ensure your child's success and happiness. Together, we can help them build a bright future.

Warm regards,

[Your Name]

[Your Title]

[School Name]

Letter to Students:

Subject: Unlocking Your Potential: A Guide to Success

Dear Students,

As you continue your academic journey, I want to remind you that you are not alone in navigating the exciting yet challenging world of education, career exploration, and personal growth. The choices you make today will shape your future, and there are countless opportunities ahead of you. Here's a guide to help you stay focused, motivated, and ready for what's next.

Choosing Your Career Path It's natural to feel uncertain about your career at this stage, and that's okay. Take time to explore different fields, discover what excites you, and develop the skills that will set you up for success. Whether it's through internships, part-time jobs, or simply talking to professionals, try to get hands-on experience in areas that interest you. Remember, your career path can change, and that's part of the journey.

Managing Your Time Effectively School can be demanding, and balancing your responsibilities may seem difficult at times. Developing good time management skills is one of the most important things you can do for your success. Organize your tasks, break them into manageable steps, and remember to make time for relaxation and hobbies. Consistency, balance, and self-care will help you stay on track and reduce stress.

Preparing for College or Future Career The college application process can be overwhelming, but staying organized and ahead of deadlines is key. Research the colleges or programs that interest you, gather all necessary documents, and make sure your application reflects your strengths and passions. Don't forget to seek advice from your teachers or a counselor if you need help navigating this process.

Building Your Resume Whether you're applying for a job, internship, or volunteering position, creating a solid resume will set you apart. Highlight your skills, academic achievements, volunteer work, and any leadership roles you've held. Don't worry if you don't have formal work experience—there are many other ways to showcase your abilities and passion.

Stay Focused and Motivated There will be challenges along the way, but it's important to stay focused on your goals. Set clear objectives, keep track of your progress, and be open to feedback. Surround yourself with supportive friends, family, and mentors who can guide you when you need it.

Remember, the journey to success is unique for each of you. Stay curious, keep learning, and embrace new opportunities as they come. You have the power to shape your future, and I'm here to support you every step of the way.

Best regards,

[Your Name]

[Your Title]

[School Name]

These letters aim to inform and motivate both parents and students by addressing common concerns and providing guidance on how to foster a supportive educational environment. Would you like to customize these letters further for specific needs?

India is home to some of the best colleges across various fields of study, known for their academic excellence, infrastructure, and strong alumni networks. Below is a list of top colleges in India, categorized by discipline:

Top Engineering Colleges

1. **Indian Institute of Technology (IIT) Bombay**
2. Location: Mumbai, Maharashtra
3. IIT Bombay is consistently ranked as one of the best engineering colleges in India, known for its excellent faculty, research, and industry connections.
4. **Indian Institute of Technology (IIT) Delhi**
5. Location: New Delhi
6. IIT Delhi is renowned for its academic rigor and strong industry connections, particularly in the fields of technology and engineering.
7. **Indian Institute of Technology (IIT) Madras**
8. Location: Chennai, Tamil Nadu
9. IIT Madras is highly regarded for its cutting-edge research and high placement rates.

10. **Indian Institute of Technology (IIT) Kharagpur**
11. Location: Kharagpur, West Bengal
12. One of the oldest IITs, known for its top-notch infrastructure and large campus.
13. **Indian Institute of Technology (IIT) Kanpur**
14. Location: Kanpur, Uttar Pradesh
15. IIT Kanpur is famous for its strong academic programs, research facilities, and global collaborations.

Top Medical Colleges

1. **All India Institute of Medical Sciences (AIIMS)**
2. Location: New Delhi
3. AIIMS is one of the most prestigious medical institutions in India, offering undergraduate and postgraduate medical education and research.
4. **Christian Medical College (CMC)**
5. Location: Vellore, Tamil Nadu
6. CMC is known for its world-class healthcare education and a high standard of clinical practice.
7. **Post Graduate Institute of Medical Education and Research (PGIMER)**
8. Location: Chandigarh

9. PGIMER is a leading institute for postgraduate medical education, research, and patient care.

10. **King George's Medical University (KGMU)**

11. Location: Lucknow, Uttar Pradesh

12. Known for its excellence in medical education and clinical practice.

13. **Kasturba Medical College**

14. Location: Manipal, Karnataka

15. KMC Manipal is a highly reputed medical college, especially for its state-of-the-art infrastructure and research.

Top Law Colleges

1. **National Law School of India University (NLSIU)**

2. Location: Bangalore, Karnataka

3. NLSIU is India's leading law school, known for its rigorous curriculum and strong alumni network.

4. **National Academy of Legal Studies and Research (NALSAR)**

5. Location: Hyderabad, Telangana

6. NALSAR is one of the top law schools in India, producing some of the best legal minds.

7. **National Law University (NLU), Delhi**

8. Location: New Delhi

9. NLU Delhi is highly ranked for its quality of education and infrastructure.
10. **The West Bengal National University of Juridical Sciences (WBNUJS)**
11. Location: Kolkata, West Bengal
12. Known for its academic excellence and strong industry connections in law.
13. **National Law University (NLU), Jodhpur**
14. Location: Jodhpur, Rajasthan
15. NLU Jodhpur has a strong reputation for its law courses and international collaborations.

Top Business Schools

1. **Indian Institute of Management (IIM) Ahmedabad**
2. Location: Ahmedabad, Gujarat
3. IIM Ahmedabad is regarded as the best business school in India, known for its top-tier MBA programs and placement records.
4. **Indian Institute of Management (IIM) Bangalore**
5. Location: Bangalore, Karnataka
6. IIM Bangalore is well-known for its global collaborations and high-quality management education.
7. **Indian Institute of Management (IIM) Calcutta**

8. Location: Kolkata, West Bengal
9. IIM Calcutta is known for its excellence in both academics and placement records.
10. **Indian School of Business (ISB)**
11. Location: Hyderabad, Telangana
12. ISB offers world-class business education, with a strong emphasis on leadership development.
13. **XLRI Xavier School of Management**
14. Location: Jamshedpur, Jharkhand
15. Known for its strong focus on management and HR studies, XLRI is one of the top private business schools in India.

Top Humanities and Social Sciences Colleges

1. **University of Delhi (DU)**
2. Location: New Delhi
3. DU is a prestigious university with a strong reputation in social sciences, arts, and humanities.
4. **Tata Institute of Social Sciences (TISS)**
5. Location: Mumbai, Maharashtra
6. TISS is renowned for its programs in social work, human resources, and development studies.
7. **Jamia Millia Islamia (JMI)**
8. Location: New Delhi

9. JMI is recognized for its excellence in humanities, social sciences, and law.
10. **Jawaharlal Nehru University (JNU)**
11. Location: New Delhi
12. JNU is known for its robust research programs in social sciences, humanities, and international studies.
13. **Banaras Hindu University (BHU)**
14. Location: Varanasi, Uttar Pradesh
15. BHU is a top university offering a range of humanities programs and has a global reputation for academic excellence.

Top Arts and Design Colleges

1. **National Institute of Design (NID)**
2. Location: Ahmedabad, Gujarat
3. NID is one of the premier design schools in India, known for its creative programs and world-class design education.
4. **Delhi College of Art (DCA)**
5. Location: New Delhi
6. DCA is a leading institute for fine arts and design, offering various undergraduate and postgraduate programs.
7. **Srishti School of Art, Design, and Technology**
8. Location: Bangalore, Karnataka

9. Known for its innovative approach to design education, Srishti is one of the top design colleges in India.

10. Pearl Academy

11. Location: New Delhi

12. Pearl Academy offers excellent programs in fashion, design, and business.

13. MIT Institute of Design

14. Location: Pune, Maharashtra

15. MIT Pune offers some of the best design programs in India, with state-of-the-art facilities.

These institutions are recognized for their high academic standards, industry connections, and strong alumni networks. Admission to many of these colleges is highly competitive and requires excellent performance in entrance exams.

Thank You for Reading my Book

I hope it was helpful to you

Leave your suggestions and feedback on my email id

divyammajhi@gmail.com

Visit my Website : www.destinycraafters.com